American Red Cross
CPR for the
Professional Rescuer
Instructor's Manual

Dedicated to Publishing Excellence

Acknowledgments

This *American Red Cross CPR for the Professional Rescuer Instructor's Manual* was developed and produced through a joint effort of the American Red Cross and the Mosby-Year Book Publishing Company.

Members of the development team at American Red Cross national headquarters responsible for developing and writing this instructor's manual included: Lawrence D. Newell, EdD, NREMT-P, project manager, writer, and instructional designer; S. Elizabeth White, MAEd, ATC, writer, instructional designer, art and design director; Martha F. Beshers, Elizabeth Buoy-Morrissey, MPH, and Robert T. Ogle, associates; Sandra D. Buesking, Lori M. Compton, Marian F. H. Kirk, and O. Paul Stearns, analysts; and Jane Moore and Juliana Stover, desktop publishers. Administrative support was provided by Denise Beale.

The following American Red Cross national headquarters Health and Safety volunteer and paid staff provided guidance and review: Robert F. Burnside, director; Frank Carroll, deputy regional director, Mid-Atlantic Regional Office; Susan J. White, marketing specialist; Kathleen Cole Oberlin, senior associate, Operations; Stephen Silverman, EdD, national volunteer consultant, Health and Safety.

The Mosby Lifeline publishing team based in Hanover, Maryland, included: David Culverwell, vice president and publisher; Richard Weimer, executive editor; Claire Merrick, executive editor; and Dana Battaglia, assistant editor.

Guidance and review were provided by members of the American Red Cross CPR/First Aid Advisory Group—1992–1993:

Sergeant Ray Cranston, committee chairperson, commanding officer, Traffic Safety Unit, Farmington Hills Police Department, Farmington Hills, Michigan

Larry Bair, director, Health and Safety and Tissue Services, Central Iowa Chapter, Des Moines, Iowa

John E. Hendrickson, director, Safety and Health, Mid-America Chapter, Chicago, Illinois

Andra Jones, director, Health and Safety, Central Mississippi Chapter, Jackson, Mississippi

Sherri Olson-Roberts, director, Health and Safety, Washtenaw County Chapter, Ann Arbor, Michigan

James A. Otte, chairman, Health and Safety Committee, Glyn County Chapter, Brunswick, Georgia

Teresita B. Ramirez, Centex County Chapter, lecturer, Department of Curriculum and Instruction, The University of Texas at Austin, Austin, Texas

W. Douglas Round, captain, Greely Fire Department, Colorado Territory, Greely, Colorado

Natalie Lynne Smith, MS, Greater Hartford Chapter, teacher, Capital Region Education Council, Alternative Vocational School, Glastonbury, Connecticut

Linda S. Wenger, director, Health and Safety, Lancaster County Chapter, Lancaster, Pennsylvania

David J. Wurzer, PhD, Greater Long Beach Chapter, Long Beach, California

Guidance and review were also provided by members of the American Red Cross First Aid Advisory Committee—1990–1991:

Frank P. Cooley, EMT-P, subcommittee chairperson, coordinator–EMS, City of Des Moines Fire Department, Des Moines, Iowa

Pamela D. Alesky, R-EMT, health services director, Greater Erie County Chapter, American Red Cross, Erie, Pennsylvania

Carol L. Belmont, RN, BES, consultant, Organization Dynamics, Inc., Burlington, Massachusetts,

Ricky Davidson, EMT-P, chief of EMS, Shreveport Fire Department, Shreveport, Louisiana

Rodney L. Dennison, EMT-P, EMS program manager, Texas Department of Health, Region I, Temple, Texas

Lance J. Kohn, Sr., EMT-P, coordinator/senior instructor, Town of Tonawanda Police Department, Tonawanda, New York

David W. Lewis, safety services director, Dallas Area Chapter, American Red Cross, Dallas, Texas

Rafael A. Ortiz, EMT-P, fire fighter, Los Angeles County Fire Department, Long Beach, California

External review was provided by the following organizations:

American College of Emergency Physicians, Dallas, Texas

International Association of Fire Fighters, Washington, D.C.

National Association of EMS Physicians, Pittsburgh, Pennsylvania

National Association of Emergency Medical Technicians, Kansas City, Missouri

National Athletic Trainers Association, Dallas, Texas

National Council of State EMS Training Coordinators, Lexington, Kentucky

United States Air Force Pararescue Association, Albuquerque, New Mexico

External review was also provided by the following individuals:

Robert S. Behnke, HSD, professor of physical education, Indiana State University, Terre Haute, Indiana

John L. Beckman, EMT-P, fire fighter, Lincolnwood Fire Department, Lincolnwood, Illinois

Clinton L. Buchanan, chief, EMS Bureau, Memphis Fire Department, Memphis, Tennessee

John J. Clair, National Ski Patrol System, Inc., Albany, New York

Rod Compton, MEd, ATC, sports medicine director, Assistant Professor, Sports Medicine Division, East Carolina University, Greenville, North Carolina

Sherman K. Sowby, PhD, CHES, professor of health science, California State University at Fresno, Fresno, California

Mary Ann Talley, program director, EMS Education, University of South Alabama, Mobile, Alabama

Bill Vargas, president, USAF Pararescue Association, Albuquerque, New Mexico

Gary W. Waites, EMT-P, EMSC, EMS course coordinator, College of the Mainland, emergency response coordinator, Amoco Corporation, Alvin, Texas

Master Sergeant Edward C. Washborn, USAF EMT program manager, 3790th Medical Service Training Wing, Sheppard AFB, Texas

Gene Weatherall, chief, Bureau of Emergency Management, Texas Department of Health, Austin, Texas

Katherine H. West, BSN, MSEd, CIC, consultant, Infection Control/Emerging Concepts Inc., Springfield, Virginia

Michael D. Zemany, AEMT/3, deputy director, North County Community College, Mt. Lakes Regional EMS Programs, Sarana Lake, New York

Contents

Part A: Administration

1 INTRODUCTION

This manual is intended to serve as a resource for instructors of the American Red Cross CPR for the Professional Rescuer course. The information and teaching suggestions it provides will help you teach the course. You should be familiar with the material in the *American Red Cross CPR for the Professional Rescuer* participant manual (Stock No. 652048) and in this instructor's manual before you teach the course.

Purpose of the Course

The purpose of the American Red Cross CPR for the Professional Rescuer course is to provide the professional rescuer with the knowledge and skills necessary in an emergency to help sustain life, reduce pain, and minimize the consequences of respiratory and cardiac emergencies until more advanced medical help can arrive.

The course content and activities will prepare participants to make appropriate decisions about the care to provide in an emergency. The course teaches the skills a professional rescuer needs to act as a crucial link in the emergency medical services (EMS) system.

Course Objectives

It is your responsibility as an instructor to see that participants meet the learning objectives listed at the beginning of each chapter in the participant manual and in this manual. At the conclusion of this course, participants should be able to—

◆ Explain how the EMS system works and how the professional rescuer's role in the EMS system differs from a citizen responder's role.
◆ Identify guidelines to follow to ensure personal safety and the safety of others at an emergency scene.
◆ Explain what happens in the body if certain body systems fail to function.
◆ Identify ways in which diseases are transmitted and describe basic safety precautions to prevent transmission.
◆ Explain the four emergency action principles.

◆ Recognize breathing emergencies, such as choking, and provide proper care for them.
◆ Identify a resuscitation mask and a bag-valve mask and demonstrate how to use them.
◆ Identify the major risk factors for cardiovascular disease and describe how to control them.
◆ Recognize the signs and symptoms of a possible heart attack, and describe how to care for someone who is experiencing persistent chest pain and/or other signs and symptoms of heart attack.
◆ Recognize the signs and symptoms of cardiac arrest, and demonstrate how to provide cardiopulmonary resuscitation (CPR).
◆ Explain how to give CPR in certain special situations and under certain conditions.

Purpose and Format of the Instructor's Manual

This instructor's manual contains all the information necessary to conduct the American Red Cross CPR for the Professional Rescuer course. The manual is divided into three parts—Part A, Administration; Part B, Teaching Tools; and Part C, Appendixes.

Part A, Administration, contains information needed to conduct the course. It provides a course overview, tells how to set up and teach the course, explains how to run practice sessions, gives requirements for successful course completion, and describes what to do when the course is completed.

Part B, Teaching Tools, includes the course outline and the lesson plans. The lesson plans provide the instructor with the primary points to be covered in each lesson and with guidelines for classroom activities.

Part C, the Appendixes, includes recommendations on manikin decontamination; final examinations A and B, answer sheets and an answer key; evaluation forms; and other materials.

Instructor's Responsibilities

Your responsibilities as an authorized Red Cross CPR for the Professional Rescuer instructor are to—
◆ Be familiar with the course materials and know how to use them effectively.
◆ Plan, coordinate, and manage the course with the local Red Cross unit.

◆ Inform participants of evaluation procedures and course completion requirements at the beginning of the course.

◆ Create a nonthreatening environment conducive to the participants' achievement of course objectives.

◆ Adapt your teaching approaches to the experience and ability of participants.

◆ Be prepared to answer participants' questions or know where to find the answers.

◆ Provide for the health and safety of participants by always ensuring that—

a. Manikins have been properly cleaned according to the recommendations in Appendix A.

b. Participants are aware of health precautions and guidelines concerning the transmission of infectious diseases and participants' physical ability to perform the skills.

c. Participants know they should consult you if they have concerns about their physical ability to perform the skills.

d. The classroom and practice areas are free of hazards.

◆ Be proficient at and able to demonstrate all the skills taught in this course.

◆ Supervise participants while they are practicing the skills.

◆ Provide participants with constructive feedback as they learn the skills.

◆ Evaluate participants' performance of skills.

◆ Identify participants who are having difficulty mastering the course materials, and develop effective strategies for raising their competence.

◆ Administer and score the final written examination.

◆ Issue course completion certificates.

◆ Submit completed course records and reports to the local Red Cross unit within the required time.

◆ Be familiar with various Red Cross courses, publications, and identification items available from the local Red Cross unit.

◆ Provide a positive example by not smoking or showing other unhealthy habits while working with participants.

◆ Identify potential instructor candidates and refer them to the appropriate Red Cross representative.

◆ Abide by the obligations in the Instructor Agreement and, if applicable, the Authorized Provider Agreement.

2 COURSE DESIGN

Course Content

The content of this course comprises information a professional rescuer needs to provide appropriate initial care for life-threatening cardiac and respiratory emergencies. The course stresses the steps to follow until more advanced life support personnel can arrive.

Course Components

The course components include a participant manual, this instructor's manual, and a video.

Participant Manual

The participant manual has been designed to facilitate the learning and understanding of the material presented in the lessons. It includes the following features:

◆ **Objectives**

At the beginning of each chapter are knowledge and skill objectives. These are the objectives the participant should be able to meet after participating in class. These objectives also appear at the beginning of each lesson in this instructor's manual. Emphasize to participants that if they can meet these objectives, they will pass the final written exam.

◆ **Key Terms**

Following the objectives is a list of defined key terms that the participant needs to know to understand chapter content. Urge participants to review their understanding of these terms while they read the chapters. A few key terms are listed in more than one chapter because they are essential to understanding the material presented in each. The pronunciation of certain medical and anatomical terms is provided, and a pronunciation guide is included in the glossary. In the chapter, key terms are printed in boldface type the first time they are explained or defined.

◆ **Sidebars**

Sidebars enhance the information in the main body of the participant manual. They present a variety of material, ranging from historical information to everyday application of the chapter's information. Sidebars add interest to the manual's content and identify unique elements that help participants better apply what they are learning.

◆ **Main Ideas**

Following the key terms is a section giving the main ideas in that chapter. Each major concept is expressed in one or two sentences.

◆ **Review Questions**

At the end of each chapter is a group of review questions designed to help participants evaluate their retention and understanding of the information in the chapter.

◆ **Figures**

Full-color photographs and illustrations throughout the manual reinforce concepts and information in each chapter.

◆ **Tables**

Tables are included in many chapters. They provide additional information and summarize important concepts.

◆ **Skill Sheets**

Illustrated skill sheets at the end of some chapters give step-by-step direction for performing certain skills shown in the video and described in those chapters. Participants use the skill sheets when they practice skills taught in the course and also for skills review.

◆ **Appendix**

Appendix A at the end of the participant manual provides additional information on a topic that may be of interest to participants—the use of automated external defibrillators.

◆ **Glossary**

The glossary defines the key terms and other words in the text that may be unfamiliar. A pronunciation guide is included. In the chapters, all terms that appear in boldface type are in the glossary. Encourage participants to consult it when they encounter an unfamiliar term.

Instructor's Manual

Lesson Plans

Several items in the lesson plans can help you conduct the course. These include—

◆ **Primary Points**

The primary points summarize the critical material—the material that is most important for the participants to understand. They also represent the information participants need to meet the objectives and pass the final written exam.

   In addition, there are notes in the lesson plans in italicized print. These notes provide specific information, expected participant responses, or clarification on certain points in the lesson plans.

◆ **Activities**

Skill practice comprises the majority of class activities. Using the video to provide skill demonstrations alleviates the need for long lectures and discussions and for the instructor to provide skill demonstrations.

◆ **Skill Practice**

In skill practice sessions, participants practice the skill either on one another or on manikins. Practice on a "real-life" victim is important to give participants experience in handling a real person. Skills that require mouth-to-mouth contact, however, such as rescue breathing, CPR, and chest or abdominal thrusts are practiced only on manikins.

Written Examinations

Two 50-question exams, A and B, are included in Appendix B of this manual. Two exams are provided so that one or the other may be used for a make-up exam. Give either exam A or exam B. Participants must pass the exam with a minimum score of 80 percent as part of the requirements for receiving an American Red Cross course completion certificate. The questions have been selected to test the participants' ability to meet the course objectives. Other questions should not be substituted.

Participant Evaluation

This course is designed to allow evaluation of the participants' skills and knowledge. Evaluation serves several purposes. It allows participants to see how much they have learned and in what areas they may be deficient. Evaluation allows the instructor to better assess the strengths and weaknesses of the participants and to address any inadequacies. Evaluation also provides the instructor with a way to assess the effectiveness of his or her teaching and of the course. Chapter 5 of this instructor's manual contains specific information on how to evaluate participants' skills and knowledge.

Video

A video has been specifically designed for this course. It is the primary vehicle for presenting course content. It includes two emergency situations in real-life settings and provides model demonstrations of all skills participants will learn.

Since many of the skills and practice sessions build on each other, you should not change the order in which the video segments are shown and skills are practiced. Do not substitute or add other videos. The only time you should not use this video is if the equipment malfunctions.

3 SETTING UP AND RUNNING THIS COURSE

Course Participants

Most of the participants will be preparing for a job that requires a professional rescuer background. Participants will include traditional public safety personnel, such as law enforcement and fire suppression personnel; medical personnel, such as EMTs, nurses, and physicians; also business/industry emergency response team members, ski patrol, lifeguards, athletic trainers, and others with a duty to respond. They may be taking the course to fulfill employment requirements, to complete requirements for a major area of study or certification, or for personal satisfaction. There are **no** prerequisites for enrollment in this course.

Health Requirements for Course Participants

The American Red Cross has a responsibility to safeguard the health and safety of participants enrolled in any Red Cross course. The materials and procedures for teaching this course have been written to reflect this concern.

As an American Red Cross instructor, one of your responsibilities is to protect participants from health risks. The procedures outlined in this manual are designed to—
- Limit the risk of transmission of communicable diseases.
- Limit the risk of one participant injuring another when practicing on a partner.
- Limit the risk that the strenuous activity involved in practice could cause injury or sudden illness.

When possible, prospective participants should be provided information about health requirements and safety before enrolling in the course. At the beginning of the course, participants will be instructed to read the information on health and safety on pages xiv–xv of the participant manual. Ask participants to talk to you before any practice if they doubt they can participate in the practice activity.

People with certain health conditions may wish not to take part in the practice sessions. These conditions include a history of heart attack or other heart conditions, respiratory problems, or other physical limitations. Suggest that these participants check with their

11

personal physician before participating in practice sessions involving physical activity. The American Red Cross advocates that, whenever possible, participants' activity levels should be adjusted as necessary to facilitate learning and help participants meet course objectives.

Tell people who take the course but cannot demonstrate the skills taught in the practice sessions that they cannot be given an American Red Cross course completion certificate. However, encourage them to participate to whatever extent possible. They can read the textbook, watch skill practice, and otherwise participate in class activities.

Course Length

The CPR for the Professional Rescuer course is designed to be completed in nine hours. It is recommended that it be taught in two or more sessions.

Recommended Class Size

The course outline and lesson plans have been developed for a class of approximately 6 to 10 participants. If your class is larger, you will probably need to allow more time or have co-instructors or instructor aides to help you. The amount of available equipment, such as manikins, may limit class size. Personal supervision is necessary to ensure effective practice and the safety of participants. If the class is too large, you may not be able to provide proper supervision or complete class activities in the allotted time.

Use of Instructor Aides

Instructor aides can help you with some parts of a course and may help you use class time more efficiently. They may have an interest in becoming instructors. It is your responsibility to ensure instructor aides who assist with the class are trained. Before allowing an instructor aide to assist you, ask to see the aide's *Instructor Aide* certificate (Cert. 3003) and a current course certificate for the course you are teaching.

The duties and responsibilities of instructor aides will vary depending on the aide's experience and ability. These duties should be limited to—

◆ Handling registration and record keeping.
◆ Setting up the classrooms and handing out supplies.

◆ Assisting with equipment (for example, setting up the VCR and monitor or an overhead projector or cleaning manikins).
◆ Helping participants with practice activities (for example, finding practice partners).
◆ Scoring written tests.

Instructor aides may help participants during the practice sessions. Before allowing this, however, make sure that the aide can demonstrate the skills correctly and guide participants effectively.

Contact your local Red Cross unit for specific information regarding its training program for instructor aides. Aide training includes discussion of—
◆ Course objectives, both knowledge objectives (what the participant needs to know and be able to do to pass the written test) and skill objectives (what the participant needs to be able to do to pass the skill tests).
◆ Course materials and their use.
◆ Course administration and scheduling.
◆ Procedures for practice sessions.
◆ Relative responsibilities of the instructor and the aide.

Classroom Environment

The classroom should provide a safe, comfortable, and appropriate learning environment. The room should be well-lighted and well-ventilated and comfortable in temperature. The classroom should have enough space for skill practice sessions, with a separate area for video viewing, lectures, discussions, and examinations, if possible. If the practice area is not carpeted, provide some knee protection (folded blankets or mats) for participants or allow them to bring their own padding materials. Urge participants to dress comfortably for practicing skills. The room should be convenient to restrooms and exits.

Usually, participants' chairs can be arranged in rows facing the front of the classroom. However, you also should consider the advantages of different seating arrangements or of rearranging seating during the class. Semicircular or circular arrangements may make participants feel more at ease at certain times. For example, participants may see each other more clearly while introducing themselves if they are in a circle or semicircle.

When participants are taking the final written examination, it may be better to have chairs arranged to allow everyone as much space as possible. This will help to reduce distractions. When participants are practicing, they may need to push their chairs against the wall to gain more floor space. Whatever seating arrangements you select, make sure that all participants can adequately see the monitor or screen when you use audiovisual materials or present skill demonstrations.

To prevent injury, do not ask participants to move heavy equipment and furniture. If you need their help to move lighter items, be sure that two or more participants move these items and use proper lifting techniques—lifting with the legs and keeping the back straight.

Course Components

The following items can be ordered from your local Red Cross unit or from Mosby-Year Book:
◆ *American Red Cross CPR for the Professional Rescuer* participant manual (Stock No. 652048)
◆ *American Red Cross CPR for the Professional Rescuer Instructor's Manual* (Stock No. 652049)
◆ *American Red Cross CPR for the Professional Rescuer* video (Stock No. 652051)

Course completion certificates are available only through your local Red Cross unit. Only authorized American Red Cross instructors can issue certificates. Participants who successfully complete the course will receive an *American Red Cross CPR for the Professional Rescuer* certificate (Stock No. 653214)

Participant's Materials
Each participant will need a participant manual. For the written exam, each participant will need a copy of either written exam A or B and a blank answer sheet.

Instructor's Materials and Equipment
You will need a participant manual and this instructor's manual, and a 1/2 inch video cassette player and a monitor. If you are not familiar with the equipment, make arrangements for proper instruction, and practice before class. You should check all equipment to ensure that it is working properly and that you have any additional needed equipment, such as an extension cord.

Equipment and supplies needed to teach this course are available through your local Red Cross unit. Some units may have a limited supply; therefore, it is important to be aware of your unit's reservation policies. Plan early to determine the dates and times when you need certain equipment and supplies. If you depend on your local unit for equipment and supplies, you should make contact at least several weeks in advance to schedule equipment and supplies for each class session. Refer to Appendix E for a complete list of equipment and supplies you will need to teach this course.

Manikins

Adult, child, and infant manikins are required equipment for this course. A participant-to-manikin ratio of 2–to–1 or 3–to–1 is recommended. All manikins should be well maintained and working properly.

Some manikins need to be cleaned during use, as described later in this chapter and in Appendix A. Some of the newer manikins have disposable plastic bags that protrude from the mouth and cover the manikin's face. Others have individual manikin faces that are applied at the time of practice and removed after an individual has practiced a skill. Manikins should be models that can be properly decontaminated after class according to the recommendations in Appendix A. To minimize the possibility of disease transmission, these recommendations should be followed strictly.

All manikins should be inspected frequently for cracks or rips in the face which make it difficult or impossible to clean the manikin properly. **Do not use any manikin that has cracks or rips in the face.**

Manikin Decontamination Supplies

For manikins that need to be cleaned during use, you will need a decontaminating solution and a large number of gauze pads. The recommended solution is 1/4 cup of liquid chlorine bleach per gallon of tap water. This solution should be made before each class and discarded after use. Do not use scented bleach. The perfume in these bleaches may impart a taste to the plastics.

Since some people find bleach objectionable, 70 percent alcohol (isopropanol or ethanol) is suggested as an alternative. Although alcohol can kill many bacteria and viruses, there are some that it will not kill. However, if the manikin's face is scrubbed vigorously with 70 percent alcohol and a clean gauze pad, it is highly unlikely that any infectious disease will be transmitted. For more information on selecting one of these decontaminating solutions, review Appendix A.

Manikin Decontamination Procedure

During practice sessions, the manikin's face and the inside of its mouth must be cleaned after each use by participant.

For some manikins, this requires the following procedures:
1. Dry the manikin's face with a clean 4" x 4" gauze pad.
2. Wet a second clean gauze pad with decontaminating solution.
3. Squeeze excess solution from the pad.
4. Scrub the manikin's face and the inside of its mouth vigorously with the soaked pad (being careful not to tear the mouth).

5. Place the wet pad over the manikin's mouth and nose and wait 30 seconds.
6. Discard the pad and dry the manikin's face with a third clean gauze pad.

Tell participants that to keep the manikins' faces clean and free from dirt, they should not place the manikins facedown. Participants should also be asked to wash their hands and remove lipstick before practice on a manikin.

Manikin Decontamination After Class
As soon as possible after the end of each class session, all manikins should be properly cleaned. Manufacturer's recommendations should be followed regarding disassembly. The parts should be scrubbed with warm soapy water, rinsed, and decontaminated with a solution of liquid household chlorine bleach and water (1/4 cup of bleach to one gallon of water). Vigorous scrubbing with soap and water is as important as scrubbing with bleach. Disposable gloves and protective eyewear should be worn while manikins are being decontaminated.

To decontaminate the manikins after class, you will need, besides the decontamination solution and gauze pads, a baby bottle brush, soap and water, basins or buckets, nonsterile disposable gloves, and any other supplies that may be recommended by the manikin manufacturer. The manikin's body, hair, and clothes should be washed periodically to ensure that the manikins are clean.

Cleaning the Resuscitation Masks After Class
Manufacturer's instructions for cleaning the resuscitation masks should be followed after each use.

Usually, the disposable one-way valve on the resuscitation mask can be cleaned and reused after practice on a manikin. For use on a victim, the disposable one-way valve should not be reused.

The resuscitation mask and one-way valve may be cleaned after training by first vigorously scrubbing in warm soapy water and rinsing with clean water. Both are then submerged for 10 minutes in a solution of water and liquid chlorine bleach (one-quarter cup of liquid chlorine bleach to one gallon of water). They are then rinsed with clean water and allowed to dry. The mask should not be pasteurized, boiled, or steamed (autoclaved).

4 HOW TO RUN PRACTICE SESSIONS

During the practice sessions, participants are learning and perfecting skills. You must decide how best to design the practice sessions. The sessions should include direction and instruction, ample practice time, instructor reinforcement, corrective feedback, and encouragement to ensure participants' success. Plan the practice sessions to reinforce the following learning objectives. Participants should be able to—

♦ Describe when to summon additional, more advanced medical personnel.
♦ Demonstrate how to apply the emergency action principles to any emergency.
♦ Demonstrate how to care for victims of respiratory and cardiac emergencies.

In general, practice sessions will involve instructor-led practice and reciprocal (partner) practice. During the practice sessions, you are responsible for—

♦ Demonstrating a skill and/or guiding students through it.
♦ Keeping the practice sessions running smoothly.
♦ Providing sufficient time for all participants to practice the skill.
♦ Identifying errors promptly and providing feedback to help participants improve their skills.
♦ Encouraging participants to improve their skills.
♦ Checking each student for skill competency. (See Chapter 5 of this manual.)
♦ Ensuring a safe practice environment and safety during the practice session.

Orienting Participants to Practice Sessions

In your introduction in Lesson 1, you should do the following:
♦ Review with participants the information on first aid and infectious disease on pages xiv–xv of the participant manual. Tell participants that if they have any of the health conditions listed on these pages, they should request a separate manikin. They also should refrain from physical activity if it is detrimental to their health and check with their doctor if in doubt.

- Before the first practice session, you should tell participants to do the following:
  - Remove jewelry as well as lipstick.
  - Place jewelry in a safe place such as a purse or deep pocket.
  - Have clean hands.
  - Refrain from smoking, using smokeless tobacco products, eating, chewing gum, or drinking during the practice sessions.
  - Review Health Precautions and Guidelines for the Professional Rescuer on pages xiv–xv in the participant manual.

Orienting participants to the practice sessions will help them get started more quickly and practice more efficiently. Participants will practice in groups of two or three (according to space and supplies). Some practice sessions require participants to practice on other participants. Others, such as CPR and rescue breathing, require practice only on a manikin. Emphasize to participants that for personal safety they do not practice these skills on each other.

How Participants Learn Skills

To acquire skills efficiently, participants should be supervised during practice sessions. They may need more attention during the first practice session. Carefully planning the first session and commending participants for good performance will set a positive tone for later sessions. CPR skills may be new to participants, and they may frequently require one-on-one attention. The following list of characteristics applies to skills and the way participants learn them:

- Course skills are complex. Participants often have some difficulties when they first begin.
- Skills are learned by practice. Refinements in technique take time, and immediate success in demonstrating the skill is unlikely.
- Skills require a defined sequence of movements. Participants should follow this sequence to perform the skills correctly.
- Learning times for each skill differ, since some skills are easier than others.
- Participants have different learning rates. Take individual differences into account when teaching the course.
- Skills are quickly forgotten. Regular practice improves retention of skills.

Use of Skill Sheets

A skill sheet is included in the participant manual for each skill that participants will practice and be checked on. These skill sheets identify the critical steps required to adequately perform each skill, and each critical step is illustrated. Directions for performing each step are next to the illustrations.

Some skill sheets have decision points. These points, in bold type, describe what care should be provided when certain conditions are found. For example, during the check for consciousness in the primary survey, if the victim is not breathing or the rescuer cannot tell, the rescuer should position the victim on his or her back (if necessary) and open the victim's airway, which are the next steps on the skill sheet. By reacting to various conditions, participants are better able to understand how to use a skill in an actual emergency situation.

Practice on a Partner (Reciprocal Practice)

Practice on a partner has been included to give participants experience in providing care for a real person. One participant acts as the victim while another provides care. Participants change roles so that each person in the group has a chance to practice the skill.

During partner practice, be sure participants take the following precautions so that they do not get hurt:
◆ Participants should not engage in horseplay, which can lead to injury.
◆ **Tell participants that they should not make mouth-to-mouth contact with a partner, should not give actual rescue breaths**, and should **not** perform actual abdominal thrusts or chest compressions.

Practice with a partner allows participants to practice skills at their own pace. One person performs the steps listed on the skill sheet. The partner reads the directions and observes him or her practice the skill. The partner should point out any errors.

If you choose to have participants practice with a partner, briefly demonstrate with a participant how to use this method using the skill sheets.

Practice on a Manikin

Participants must practice on a manikin to learn the complete procedures for rescue breathing, first aid for an unconscious victim with an obstructed airway, and CPR. Participants must successfully demonstrate these skills on a manikin to receive an American Red Cross course completion certificate.

Having the manikins out of their cases at the beginning of class can help save valuable class time. If you take the manikins out before class, cover each face with a shield or piece of gauze to keep it clean. If you keep the manikins in their cases until the beginning of the practice session, allow a few minutes to get them out at the beginning of the session.

Instructor-Led Practice

Instructor-led practice, or drill, can be used for speeding up skill practice. It is particularly useful for introducing new skills that build on previously learned skills, for example, adding chest compressions to rescue breathing to perform CPR.

When you lead the practice, position the participants so you can see everyone. If the participants are practicing on manikins, the manikins' heads should be pointing in the same direction and all the participants should be in the same position next to the manikins. If the participants are practicing on partners, being able to see everyone allows you to judge skill competency as well as ensure participant safety.

Read each step on the skill sheets aloud, and have participants do each step together as a group, one step at a time. For most skills, allow the participants additional time to continue practicing on their own.

Helping Participants Practice Correctly

You should watch for errors participants make while practicing. Try to correct problems as soon as possible so that participants will practice the skill correctly. While you are working closely with one participant, check others with an occasional glance. Correct any major problems you notice to keep participants from continuing to practice incorrectly. Encourage participants to ask questions if they are unsure how to perform any part of a skill. Stay in the practice area throughout the practice session to help participants who need assistance.

A positive learning environment is important. Participants perform best when they are kept informed of their progress. When they are practicing correctly, provide positive feedback. If they are practicing incorrectly, provide specific corrective feedback. But before saying what they are doing wrong, tell them what they are doing correctly. Then tactfully help them correct their errors.

Refer them to the skill sheet when appropriate. Other strategies for corrective feedback include the following:

◆ If the error is simple, explain directly and positively how to correct the skill. Be specific when providing feedback. For example, if the participant is having trouble getting the chest to rise during rescue breathing you might say, "Your hand position is good, but you should tilt the head back farther. That will open the airway more so your breaths can go in more easily."

- You may have to show the participant what he or she should be doing. For the previous example, you might have to tilt the manikin's head yourself to show the participant how far back the manikin's head should be to open the airway.
- It may help to tell the participants why they should perform a skill in a certain way. This may help them remember to perform the skill correctly. For example, if a participant continues to forget to check the pulse before giving chest compressions, you might remind the participant that the victim may have a pulse and therefore not need chest compressions.
- If a participant has an ongoing problem with technique, carefully observe what he or she is doing. Give exact instructions for performing the technique the correct way, and lead the participant through the skill. It may be helpful to the participant to repeat the steps back to you to help reinforce them correctly.

Throughout this process, you should continue to remind the participants of both what they are doing right and what they are doing wrong. Use phrases like "Your compressions are very smooth, but they should be a little deeper," or "You are doing a good job locating the pulse, but you need to feel for a pulse long enough to be sure it is present or absent." Help participants focus on the "critical" aspects for each skill, which when performed incorrectly may be life-threatening. These critical steps are in the illustrations and directions on the skill sheets.

Common Participant Errors

The following list of common errors will help you when you are watching participants work through the practice sessions. The list is intended to help you assist students in performing the skill in a way that provides mechanical advantage and ease of learning. The list is not intended to be a list of "critical errors" or criteria for passing the skill. **The criteria for passing a skill is successful completion of the steps listed on the skill sheets.**

Checking for Consciousness
- Not using a combination of tapping **and** shouting

Positioning the Victim
- Not supporting the victim's head and neck when rolling the victim
- Not rolling the victim as a single unit

Opening the Airway
◆ Not tilting the head back far enough to open the airway
◆ Forgetting to lift the chin
◆ Applying pressure on the soft parts under the chin when lifting the chin (wrong finger placement)
◆ Closing the mouth when lifting the chin
◆ Placing the hand under the neck instead of lifting the chin

Checking for Breathing
◆ Not placing the ear close enough to the mouth and nose of the victim
◆ Not looking at the chest when checking for breathing
◆ Not checking long enough for breathing

Breathing into the Victim
◆ Not pinching the nose
◆ Not making an adequate mouth-to-mouth seal, causing air to leak out around the mouth when breaths are given
◆ Giving breaths too quickly or forcefully. Each breath should be delivered slowly (for about 1 1/2 seconds) until the chest gently rises.
◆ Not watching the chest rise and fall

Checking the Pulse
◆ Not keeping the airway open while checking the pulse
◆ Checking for the pulse in the wrong place; for example, pressing on the windpipe when checking the carotid pulse.
◆ Using the thumb to check the pulse
◆ Not checking the pulse for 5 to 10 seconds

Complete Airway Obstruction (Conscious Victim)
◆ Not determining that the victim is choking
◆ Not locating the correct hand position for giving abdominal or chest thrusts
◆ Not keeping the elbows out when pretending to give abdominal thrusts

Complete Airway Obstruction (Unconscious Victim)
◆ Not retilting the head and repeating rescue breath attempts
◆ Checking the pulse before the obstruction is cleared and the rescuer is able to breathe air into the victim
◆ Not locating the correct hand position to give abdominal/chest thrusts or back blows
◆ Forgetting the foreign body check/finger sweep step

CPR
◆ Kneeling in the wrong position or place beside the victim
◆ Not properly locating hand/finger position for compressions
◆ Not relocating the proper hand position for compressions when the hands lose contact with the chest
◆ Placing the palm rather than the heel of the hand on the breastbone when giving compressions

Physically Challenged Participants

As an American Red Cross instructor, you may be asked to present this course to a class that includes one or more physically challenged participants. Physically challenged participants include those who are deaf or hard of hearing or legally blind, lack full use of limbs, or have breathing difficulties or other physical problems. In some instances, entire classes may be composed of this special group. When the physically challenged individual can meet the stated course objectives, he or she should receive a course completion certificate.

The following instructor considerations can help the physically challenged individual succeed in class:
◆ Physically challenged individuals **can learn** first aid skills, including CPR.
◆ Instructors can adapt their teaching to these individuals.
◆ There is no one strategy for teaching participants who have physical limitations.
◆ Methods of recognizing the limitations include—
   ◆ Instructor observation of participants.
   ◆ Participants' statements.

Helping Participants Overcome Physical Challenges

To help the participant overcome a physical challenge, you may modify the delivery of course materials as follows:
◆ Increase the amount of time you spend with each participant.
◆ Allow frequent rests.
◆ Help participants modify the techniques necessary for successful skill completion. For example, a participant with one arm could be instructed to seal the nose with his or her cheek while using his or her arm and hand to do the head-tilt/chin-lift in rescue breathing. Another example would be allowing a participant who is unable to get on the floor to perform skills on a manikin placed on a table or other platform.

Refer to Appendix F, The Americans With Disabilities Act—
Course Modification Guide, for more information on teaching
physically challenged individuals.

Emphasize the value of information and skills learned, regardless
of whether or not participants earn course certificates.

5 REQUIREMENTS FOR SUCCESSFUL COURSE COMPLETION

Criteria for Course Completion and Certification

On successful completion of the course, participants receive an *American Red Cross CPR for the Professional Rescuer* certificate (Stock No. 653214). To receive the course completion certificate for the American Red Cross CPR for the Professional Rescuer course, the participant must—
◆ Demonstrate competency in each skill taught in the course.
◆ Correctly answer at least 80 percent of the final examination questions.

Participants should be told of the requirements when they enroll for the course and again during the course introduction.

Course Certification

Many agencies, organizations, and individuals look to the American Red Cross for formal training resulting in CPR for the Professional Rescuer certification. Red Cross certification means that on a particular date an instructor verified that a course participant could do the following:
◆ Demonstrate competency in each skill taught in the course. This is defined as being able to perform each skill correctly without guidance.
◆ Correctly answer at least 80 percent of the questions on a final written examination.

Achieving course certification does not imply any future demonstration of the skill or knowledge at the level achieved on the particular date. Furthermore, certification does not imply any obligation to give assistance or that the assistance that would be provided would be equal to the level of performance on the date that the course was completed. Participants should be informed of the requirements for certification and what certification is when they enroll for the course and during the course introduction.

Requirements for Successful Course Completion

Evaluating Skills

Checking skill competency is an important instructor responsibility. Making accurate and consistent judgments on skill checks enables you to evaluate each participant's skills fairly. Checking each participant's competency at demonstrating each skill enables you to—

◆ Identify those participants who can correctly demonstrate the skills.

◆ Identify those who are having difficulty demonstrating the skills and arrange additional time for skill practice.

◆ Determine each participant's ability to recognize an emergency and take appropriate action.

Your judgment as to whether or not a participant can competently perform a skill plays a major role in maintaining the high quality of American Red Cross CPR for the Professional Rescuer instruction. More important, the knowledge that he or she can perform a skill competently will help build the participant's confidence in his or her ability to act appropriately in a real emergency.

Having skills checked should not be fearful or stressful for the participant. Conduct these checks in a relaxed and informal manner. Provide participants with continual feedback on their progress during the practice sessions and help them focus on the essential skill components.

You can check participants' skills individually or in small groups depending on the skill. If your class is large, you will need to use time wisely when checking skills. If you notice a participant performing a skill appropriately while working alone, with a partner or as part of a larger group, you may check him or her off on that skill. Further evaluation is not necessary. But if you are unable to observe and check off everyone in this manner, you will need to evaluate the remaining participants' skills either individually or in a small group.

When evaluating participants—

◆ Ask the participant to demonstrate the complete skill if you did not observe him or her doing so during practice. (Sometimes participants try to talk through a skill rather than perform it.)

◆ Ensure that each step on the skill sheet is performed correctly.

◆ Give only the information about the victim's condition that will prompt the participant as to the appropriate action to take next.

◆ If the participant makes a major error, such as forgetting to check breathing or pulse before starting CPR, stop the participant and point out the error.

26

◆ If the participant gives one too many compressions, allow him or her to continue. Adding or leaving out a compression has little or no impact on the effectiveness of CPR.

◆ If the error shows a basic misunderstanding of the procedure, give corrective feedback and give the participant more time to review the video and practice before checking him or her again.

◆ If the error is easily corrected, recheck the participant immediately, asking him or her to correct the mistake.

◆ After the participant has successfully demonstrated the skill, mark the successful completion of the skill on the Participant Progress Log (Appendix G of this manual).

When possible, participants should be checked off on a specific skill by the end of the lesson. If you decide that a participant cannot perform the skill properly, advise the participant that he or she needs to practice more and that you will check off the skill later. Remember that participants will have opportunities to work on these skills at other points in the course, so you can check skills at a later time. If by the end of the course a participant has not successfully completed all skill checks, withhold the certificate and suggest that the participant take the course again.

Focus on the critical skill steps such as whether the participant determines absence of breathing or pulse or whether the airway is obstructed before providing specific care. Also, make sure that the care provided was appropriate. (For example, the participant gave chest compressions only when told a pulse was absent and abdominal thrusts only when told the airway was obstructed.) Do not focus on minor issues such as whether a participant first put his or her fingers on the Adam's apple before sliding them into the groove on the side of the neck to check for a pulse. It is more important that the participant's fingers were in the right place to feel the pulse and that the participant took the time to evaluate its presence or absence before beginning chest compressions.

As another example, when a participant is giving rescue breathing, the manikin's chest should rise and fall and breaths should be given in a reasonable amount of time (every 3 to 6 seconds). It is most important that the rescuer breathes gently into the lungs and looks for chest movement rather than split-second timing. In this way, the participant will focus on the most important aspect of a skill. **The steps written on the skill sheet are the only steps necessary for successful completion of a skill.**

Requirements for Successful Course Completion

Written Examination

A final written exam is given at the end of the course to participants who have passed all the skill competency checks and want Red Cross course certification. Two 50-question exams, A and B, are in Appendix B of this manual.

Either exam A or exam B should be given as part of the requirements for receiving an American Red Cross completion certificate. Other exam questions should not be substituted. To earn certification, participants must answer at least 80 percent of the questions correctly. Participants must not refer to their manual when taking the exam.

Examination Security

Examination security is your responsibility. It is not recommended that participants be allowed to see the written exam before it is distributed. As participants hand in their answer sheets, you may quickly grade the exam and return it to the participant. This way the participant can review any incorrect answers. Be sure to collect all answer sheets and exams before the participants leave the class.

Criteria for Grading Participants—For American Red Cross Course Completion Only

If a participant passes all the skill competency checks but fails the written exam, you may give the alternate version of the exam after the participant has studied for a retest. If you think that the participant's score on the written exam was low because of poor reading skills, you may give the exam orally. In this case, enter each answer on the answer sheet and score the exam as usual. If the participant scores at least 80 percent on the retest, "Pass" (P) should be entered as the final grade.

The *American Red Cross Course Record* (Forms 6418 and 6418A) requires that you enter a grade of pass, fail, incomplete, or audit for each participant. The information below will help you assign the correct grade:

◆ **"Pass" (P)** should be entered as the final grade for a participant who has passed all the skill checks and scored at least 80 percent on the final written exam.

◆ **"Fail" (F)** should be entered as the final grade for a participant who has not passed **all** the required skill checks and/or the final written exam and prefers not to be reexamined, or who does not pass a retest.

◆ **"Incomplete" (Inc)** should be entered as the final grade if the participant is unable to complete the course because of certain circumstances, such as an illness or death in the family. An "Incomplete" is given only when arrangements to complete the training have been made.

◆ **"Audit"** should be entered as the final grade for a participant who has chosen the self-evaluation option for testing. This should not be substituted for a "Fail" for a participant who attempts certification but is unable to pass the completion requirements.

6 *COURSE CONCLUSION*

Awarding Certificates

Discuss procedures for obtaining an American Red Cross course completion certificate for participants in your course with your local Red Cross unit. Be sure to follow approved procedures. Sign the certificates before giving them to the participants. If you will be obtaining the certificates after the course is completed, you should arrange to get them to the participants. Ask participants to submit stamped, self-addressed envelopes in advance.

Participants will be awarded an *American Red Cross CPR for the Professional Rescuer* certificate (Stock No. 653214), which is valid for one year.

Reporting Procedures

At the conclusion of the course, you must complete and sign the *American Red Cross Course Record* (Form 6418 and Form 6418A) and turn it in promptly to your local Red Cross unit. It is important that you keep a copy for your records and make a copy for the institution or organization where you conducted the course. Your local unit may require that you complete other forms such as an equipment log sheet. If you have any problems with a Red Cross unit's equipment, report them to that unit.

Course Evaluation

Three evaluations are recommended to be completed at the conclusion of this course.

Participants' Evaluation
Feedback from participants is an important part of any evaluation process. Participants should have an opportunity to tell you what they thought about the course. Have them complete evaluations each time you teach this course. This information will provide you with feedback concerning the course and its instruction and help the Red Cross maintain the high quality of the course. Make copies of Appendix C, or use your local Red Cross unit's evaluation. At the

31

last session, give this form to all participants to be completed before they leave. Give these course evaluations to your local Red Cross unit, if required. Please do not forward these evaluations to national headquarters.

Instructor Evaluation

To continue to improve this course, the American Red Cross needs your help. After you teach the course the first time, use your participants' feedback to help you complete the first Instructor Evaluation form (Appendix D). Detach and return the completed evaluation (either as a self-fold mailer or by placing a copy in an envelope) to—

American Red Cross National Headquarters
Health and Safety Course Evaluation
431 18th Street, N.W.
Washington, DC 20006–5310

You will also find a second Instructor Evaluation form in Appendix D. Use the second form or write this address if you wish to share any observations or suggestions from future courses that you instruct.

Instructor Self-Assessment

You may find it useful to use the Instructor Self-Assessment and Development evaluation in Appendix H to rate your instructional skills.

Review Course

The review course outline and instructions for conducting the course challenge are in Appendix I.

Part B: Teaching Tools

Course Outline: American Red Cross
CPR for the Professional Rescuer

The course described in the following outline comprises 8 lessons. The 8th lesson includes the written exam. A complete list of the equipment and supplies needed for each lesson is in Appendix E of this manual.

Lesson Content	Video	Skill Practice	Time
1. Introduction	✔		0:30
2. Human Body Systems; Disease Transmission	✔		0:30
3. Priorities of Care	✔	✔	0:40
4. Breathing Emergencies	✔	✔	2:15
5. Breathing Devices	✔	✔	1:20
6. Cardiac Emergencies	✔	✔	2:45
7. Special Resuscitation Situations			0:15
8. Written Exam			0:45
Total			**9:00**

Lesson 1: INTRODUCTION

Length: 30 minutes

Equipment and Supplies:	Video; name tags; course roster; course outline; participant manual
Goal:	Participants will become familiar with the criteria for successful completion of this course, with how professional rescuers work within the EMS system, and with their roles and responsibilities as professional rescuers.
Knowledge Objectives:	After completing this lesson, participants will be able to—

1. List desirable characteristics of professional rescuers.
2. Describe the structure and function of the emergency medical services (EMS) system.
3. Describe the responsibilities of professional rescuers.
4. Identify nine legal considerations for professional rescuers.

INTRODUCTION TO THE COURSE

Time: 10 minutes

Activity:

1. Introduce yourself and welcome participants to the American Red Cross.
2. Have participants introduce themselves by sharing their names, their reasons for taking this course, and their expectations of the course. Provide name tags for participants to fill out.
3. Give a brief description of your background and credentials. Identify yourself as a Red Cross instructor and explain that this course is one of many offered by the American Red Cross. Ask participants to write their full name and address on the course roster so that you can complete the *American Red Cross Course Record* (Form 6418 and Form 6418A).
4. Point out the location of fire exits, telephones, restrooms, and drinking fountains, and explain classroom no smoking rule and building rules if any.
5. Tell participants to wear comfortable clothes suitable for skill practice.
6. Explain the class schedule and hand out a course outline.
7. Explain that the course is designed to provide professional rescuers with the knowledge and skills necessary in an emergency to help sustain life, reduce pain, and minimize the consequences of respiratory and cardiac emergencies until more advanced medical help arrives.

8. Explain that the material they will learn is primarily presented in a video that provides demonstrations of skills and two emergency scenarios. Participants will practice the skills either on a manikin or on a partner.

9. Identify the participant manual for this course, *American Red Cross CPR for the Professional Rescuer* (Stock No. 652048). Make sure each participant has a copy. Point out—
   ◆ Objectives.
   ◆ Key Terms.
   ◆ Main Ideas
   ◆ Sidebars.
   ◆ Figures and Tables.
   ◆ Review Questions.
   ◆ Skill Sheets.

10. Tell participants that reading the chapters and answering the Review Questions will help them understand and retain the material they learn in class.

11. Explain that to successfully complete the course, participants must—
    ◆ Correctly demonstrate all the skills taught.
    ◆ Pass a 50-question final exam with a score of 80 percent or better.

THE PROFESSIONAL RESCUER

Time: 15 minutes

Activity:

1. Tell participants they are going to view a video that defines the roles of professional rescuers in the emergency medical services (EMS) system.

Video:

Show the video segment: *The Professional Rescuer.*

Primary Points:

2. Briefly reinforce the following major points:
   ◆ The EMS system functions as a series of events linked in a chain, a chain of survival. The survival and recovery of the victim depend on this chain of events. These events include—
     ◆ Recognition of an emergency.
     ◆ Early activation of EMS.
     ◆ First responder care.
     ◆ More advanced prehospital care, such as by paramedics.
     ◆ Hospital care.
   ◆ For the EMS system to work effectively, prompt response is vital.

LEGAL CONSIDERATIONS

Time: 5 minutes

Activity:

Primary Points:

1. Point out to participants that Part 1 of their manual contains information on legal issues that professional rescuers need to be aware of. Briefly mention the following points:

    ◆ **Duty to act.** Most professional rescuers have a duty to act in an emergency.

    ◆ **Standard of care.** The public expects a certain standard of care from a professional rescuer. If your actions do not meet the standards set for you, you may be successfully sued if your actions harm another person.

    ◆ **Negligence.** Negligence is the failure to follow a reasonable standard of care, thereby causing injury to someone. A person could be negligent by acting wrongly or failing to act at all.

    ◆ **Good Samaritan laws.** Most states have Good Samaritan laws, which protect people providing emergency care. These laws differ from state to state. You should be familiar with your state's laws.

    ◆ **Consent.** Before you provide care, you must obtain the victim's consent. You must—

    ◆ Identify yourself.
    ◆ Give your level of training.
    ◆ Explain what you think must be wrong.
    ◆ Explain what you plan to do.

    A parent or guardian, if present, must give consent to care for a minor unless a life-threatening condition exists. If the victim is unconscious or too confused or upset to grant care, the law assumes the victim would grant consent if able to do so. This is called implied consent.

    ◆ **Refusal of care.** If a person refuses care, even if his or her condition is serious, you should honor the request. If possible, have someone witness the refusal. Document it; some EMS systems have a "Refusal of Care" form you can use in such situations.

    ◆ **Abandonment.** Once you have started emergency care, you are legally obligated to continue that care until a person with equal or higher training relieves you. If you stop care before that happens, you can be legally responsible for the abandonment of a person in need.

- **Confidentiality.** When providing care, protect the victim's confidentiality. Never discuss the victim or the care you gave with anyone except law enforcement personnel or personnel caring for the victim.
- **Record Keeping.** Always document your care as soon as possible. Your record may be helpful to others providing care. Your record is also a legal document and will support what you saw, heard, and did at the scene of the emergency.
- Participants should read this information in Part 1 of their participant manual and familiarize themselves with the legal concepts discussed. Since the laws vary from state to state, participants are also advised to become familiar with those of their state.
- The sidebar, "A Right to Choose," in Part 1 of the participant manual, describes another set of issues with legal implications. Participants should become familiar with these also, since they may have to deal with them at some time.

Lesson 2:
HUMAN BODY SYSTEMS; DISEASE TRANSMISSION

Length: 30 minutes

Equipment and Supplies:	Video
Goal:	Participants will become familiar with the structures, functions, and interdependence of specific body systems; they will gain a basic understanding of disease transmission and how to protect against it.
Knowledge Objectives:	After completing this lesson, participants will be able to—

1. Identify the major structures of the respiratory, circulatory, and nervous systems.
2. Describe the primary functions of these body systems.
3. Give an example of how these body systems work together.
4. Describe what can happen to the body if a problem occurs in one or more of these body systems.
5. Describe the four ways pathogens enter the body.
6. Name three ways to protect from disease transmission when giving care.

HUMAN BODY SYSTEMS

Time: 15 minutes

Primary Points:

◆ Knowing how the respiratory, circulatory, and nervous systems normally function will help you understand what happens when these systems fail.

◆ When body systems fail, physical signs and symptoms appear. These are often your first indication that something is wrong.

Video: Show the video: *Human Body Systems.*

Primary Points:

◆ Body systems have unique structures and functions.

◆ **Respiratory System:** (nose, mouth, epiglottis, trachea, lungs, bronchi, alveoli, diaphragm; brings oxygen into the body in inhaled air, exchanges oxygen with carbon dioxide, and removes carbon dioxide from body in exhaled air.)

◆ **Circulatory System:** (arteries, veins, capillaries, heart; pumps oxygen-rich blood throughout the body, carries oxygen-poor blood back to the heart.)

◆ **Nervous System:** (brain, spinal cord, nerves; regulates all body functions including respiratory and circulatory systems.)

◆ Body systems work together to keep the body healthy. They do not work independently.

◆ Injury or illness rarely affect only one body system. For example, if the heart stops beating, breathing will stop. If the body is deprived of oxygen, brain cells will begin to die within 4 to 6 minutes.

DISEASE TRANSMISSION

Time: 15 minutes

Activity:

Primary Points:

1. Tell participants to read Chapter 3, Disease Transmission, in their manual on their own time and answer the Review Questions. Briefly discuss the following points:

◆ Diseases are caused by microorganisms called pathogens.

◆ Pathogens enter the body in four ways:

   ◆ By direct contact with an infected person's body fluids, such as blood or saliva

   ◆ By indirect contact—touching an object with contaminated body fluids on it

   ◆ By inhaling infected droplets in the air

   ◆ By being bitten by an infected animal or insect

◆ Herpes, meningitis, tuberculosis, hepatitis, and HIV, the virus that causes AIDS, are serious diseases that must be of concern to professional rescuers.

◆ You can protect yourself from disease transmission by following certain precautions when giving care, such as wearing protective coverings—gloves and masks, using a resuscitation mask for rescue breathing, getting appropriate immunizations, and following certain work control practices that change the way a task is carried out. Examples of work control practices include—

   ◆ Not trying to bend or recap any needles.

   ◆ Removing soiled protective clothing as soon as possible. Washing hands thoroughly immediately after providing care. Cleaning and disinfecting all equipment and work surfaces possibly soiled by blood or other body fluids.

◆ If you think you have been exposed to an infectious disease, it is your responsibility to notify your supervisor immediately. You should receive medical evaluation, counseling, and postexposure care.

Lesson 3: PRIORITIES OF CARE

Length: 40 minutes

Equipment and Supplies:	Video; Skill Sheet "Primary Survey"; Participant Progress Log; blankets or mats
Goal:	Participants will become familiar with how and when to perform a primary survey.
Knowledge Objectives:	After completing this lesson, participants will be able to—
	1. Describe the four emergency action principles.
	2. Explain why you do a primary survey in every emergency situation.
	3. Describe how to do a primary survey.
Skill Objectives:	After completing the class, participants will be able to—
	1. Demonstrate how to do a primary survey.
	2. Make appropriate decisions about care when given an example of an emergency requiring them to do a primary survey.

EMERGENCY ACTION PRINCIPLES

Time: 15 minutes

Primary Points:

- The four emergency action principles are—
  - Survey the scene.
  - Do a primary survey.
  - Summon additional personnel if necessary.
  - Do a secondary survey.

The Primary Survey

Video: Show the video segment: *Primary Survey.*

Primary Points:

- The primary survey identifies life-threatening conditions.
- The four items to check in the primary survey are—
  - Consciousness.
  - Airway.
  - Breathing.
  - Circulation (pulse and severe bleeding).
- The primary survey can be done with the victim in the position in which you find him or her. If, however, you are unsure whether a face-down victim is breathing, position the victim on the back.
- A person who is speaking or crying is conscious, has an open airway, is breathing, and has a pulse.

43

◆ Sometimes the tongue is blocking the airway. The head-tilt/
chin-lift technique opens the airway by moving the tongue
away from the back of the throat.

◆ Open the airway to check for breathing.

◆ If the victim is not breathing but has a pulse, do rescue
breathing.

◆ A person who makes no sound and fails to respond to
stimulation may be unconscious and possibly not breathing
and/or without a pulse.

SKILL PRACTICE: PRIMARY SURVEY

Time: 25 minutes

Activity:

Positioning the Victim Faceup

1. Ask participants to take skill sheets with them to the
practice area.
2. Assign partners or ask participants to find partners.
3. Tell participants that they will practice positioning a
victim, using their partner to simulate a face-down,
unconscious victim.
4. Guide participants through the skill.
5. After participants have practiced positioning the victim to
the point at which they feel comfortable in their ability to
perform the skill, have participants change places. Repeat
the practice. Check off participants' skills as you watch
them practice.
6. Answer any questions.

Activity:

Primary Survey

1. Tell the participants that they will practice the primary survey
on an unconscious but breathing victim.

*Note: Participants will tilt the head back and lift the chin to
open the victim's airway. Then check for breathing. Since the
victim is breathing, the rescuer does not need to check the
carotid pulse but will check for severe bleeding.*

2. Have participants practice performing a primary survey on an
unconscious victim who is not breathing.

*Note: In this situation, participants should be told that they
would give 2 slow breaths for the nonbreathing person and then
do a pulse check and bleeding check. This is because the
nonbreathing adult victim is likely to be pulseless.*

3. Guide participants through the skill. Have participants locate their own carotid pulse and then locate their partner's carotid pulse.
4. After participants have practiced the skills to the point at which they feel comfortable with their ability to perform them, have the participants change places. Repeat the practice. Check off participants' skills as you watch them practice.
5. Answer any questions.

Lesson 4: BREATHING EMERGENCIES

Length: 2 hours, 15 minutes

Equipment and Supplies: Video; Skill Sheets: "Rescue Breathing for an Adult," "Rescue Breathing for an Infant," "Care for an Unconscious Adult/Child with an Obstructed Airway," "Care for a Conscious Adult/Child with an Obstructed Airway," "Care for an Unconscious Infant with an Obstructed Airway," "Care for a Conscious Infant with an Obstructed Airway"; Participant Progress Log; adult and infant manikins (child manikins optional); decontamination supplies; blankets or mats

Goal: Participants will become familiar with how to respond to a breathing emergency in an adult, in a child, and in an infant.

Knowledge Objectives: After completing this lesson, participants will be able to—
1. List the signs and symptoms of respiratory distress.
2. Describe how to care for a victim of respiratory distress.
3. Explain when to provide rescue breathing.
4. Describe how to provide rescue breathing.
5. List three causes of an obstructed airway.
6. Describe how to care for an unconscious adult, child, and infant victim with an obstructed airway.
7. Describe how to care for a conscious adult, child, and infant victim with an obstructed airway.

Skill Objectives: After completing the class, participants will be able to—
1. Demonstrate rescue breathing for an adult, a child, and an infant.
2. Demonstrate how to care for an unconscious adult, child, and infant with an obstructed airway.
3. Demonstrate how to care for a conscious adult, child, and infant with an obstructed airway.
4. Make appropriate decisions about care when given an example of an emergency in which a person is not breathing.

RECOGNIZING BREATHING EMERGENCIES

Time: 5 minutes

Respiratory Distress

Primary Points:
◆ Someone having trouble breathing is said to be in respiratory distress.
◆ Causes of breathing emergencies:
  ◆ Heart attack or heart disease
  ◆ Lung disease, such as emphysema
  ◆ Asthma
  ◆ Injury to the chest or lungs
  ◆ Allergic reactions to food, drugs, and insect bites or stings
  ◆ Drowning or near drowning
  ◆ Electrocution
  ◆ Poisoning
  ◆ Shock
◆ Signs and symptoms of respiratory distress:
  ◆ Gasping for air
  ◆ Unusually fast or slow breathing
  ◆ Unusually shallow or deep breathing
  ◆ Unusually noisy breathing
  ◆ Painful breathing
  ◆ Dizziness
  ◆ Feeling short of breath
  ◆ Tingling in the hands or feet
  ◆ Moist, pale, bluish, or flushed skin

CARING FOR BREATHING EMERGENCIES

Time: 15 minutes

Care for Respiratory Distress

Primary Points:
◆ Position person in a sitting position.
◆ Attempt to reduce heat if room is hot and stuffy.
◆ Administer supplemental oxygen when it is available.

Respiratory Arrest

Primary Points:
◆ Respiratory distress, if uncared for, can turn into respiratory arrest.
◆ Respiratory arrest is a life-threatening condition in which breathing stops.
◆ It is commonly caused by injury, illness, or choking.
◆ In respiratory arrest, body systems will fail because of lack of oxygen.

	Care for Respiratory Arrest
Primary Points:	◆ Rescue breathing is the care you provide for a person who is in respiratory arrest but has pulse.
Video:	Show the video segment: *Rescue Breathing.*
Primary Points:	◆ Start by checking a victim's consciousness, then the ABCs.
	◆ Sometimes the tongue is blocking the airway. The head-tilt/chin-lift technique opens the airway by moving the tongue away from the back of the throat.
	◆ Open the airway to check for breathing. If the victim is not breathing, give 2 breaths. Blow in slowly until the chest rises.
	◆ Check for a pulse. If a pulse is present but the victim is still not breathing, continue rescue breathing.
	◆ For adults, give 1 breath every 5 seconds. For children and infants, give 1 breath every 3 seconds.
	◆ Give rescue breathing for 1 minute, then recheck the pulse.
	◆ For an infant, make a seal with your mouth over both the nose and mouth of the infant when you give breaths.

SKILL PRACTICE: RESCUE BREATHING
(adult, child, infant)

Time: 30 minutes

Activity:	1. Briefly review the "Health Precautions and Guidelines for the Professional Rescuer."
	2. Explain that participants will practice rescue breathing on a manikin.
	3. Demonstrate how to properly clean the manikin after use. Tell them to keep the manikin on its back at all times in order to keep the face clean.
	4. Ask the participants to take their skill sheets to the practice area.
	5. Assign partners or ask participants to find partners.
	6. Guide participants through the skill.
	7. After participants have practiced the skill to the point at which they feel comfortable in their ability to perform it, have participants change places. Repeat the practice. Check off participants' skills as you watch them practice.
	8. Answer any questions.

AIRWAY OBSTRUCTION

Time: 10 minutes

Primary Points:

- ◆ Airway obstruction is the most common respiratory emergency.
- ◆ There are two types of airway obstruction—anatomical and mechanical.
- ◆ An obstruction is called anatomical if the airway is blocked by an anatomical structure such as the tongue or swollen tissues of the mouth and throat.
- ◆ The most common cause of obstruction in an unconscious person is the tongue, which drops to the back of the throat and blocks the airway.
- ◆ An obstruction is called mechanical if the airway is blocked by a foreign object, such as a piece of food, a small toy, or fluids such as vomit, blood, mucus, or saliva. Someone with a mechanical obstruction is said to be choking.
- ◆ A person who is choking may have either a complete or a partial airway obstruction.
- ◆ A person with a partial airway obstruction can still move air to and from the lungs, which enables him or her to be able to cough in an attempt to dislodge the object.
- ◆ A person with a complete airway obstruction is unable to speak, breathe, or cough.

First Aid for Airway Obstruction

Video:

Show the video segment: *Clearing an Obstructed Airway— Adult and Child.*

Primary Points:

- ◆ The head-tilt/chin-lift technique opens the airway by moving the tongue away from the back of the throat. If the airway is blocked by a foreign object, attempt to remove it by giving abdominal thrusts (the Heimlich maneuver).
- ◆ Care for an obstructed airway for a child in the same way as for an adult, but give the thrusts with less force.

SKILL PRACTICE: OBSTRUCTED AIRWAY

Time: 30 minutes

Activity:

Conscious Adult and Child

1. Ask participants to take skill sheets with them to the practice area.
2. Explain that participants will practice how to care for a conscious victim whose airway is obstructed on their partner, but they will not give actual abdominal thrusts.
3. Have participants stand in a line or semi-circle with their partner behind them.
4. Guide participants through the skill.
5. After participants have practiced the skill to the point at which they feel comfortable in their ability to perform it, have the participants change places. Repeat the practice. Check off participants' skills as you watch them practice.
6. Answer any questions.

Unconscious Adult and Child

1. Assign partners or ask participants to find partners.
2. Tell the participants that they will use a manikin to practice first aid for an unconscious adult and an unconscious child whose airway is obstructed.
3. Guide the participants through the skill.
4. After participants have practiced the skills to the point at which they feel comfortable in their ability to perform them, have the participants change places. Repeat the practice. Check off participants' skills as you watch them practice.

AIRWAY OBSTRUCTION FOR INFANTS

Time: 10 minutes

Video:

Show the video segment: *Clearing an Obstructed Airway: Infant.*

Primary Points:

◆ Care for infants who are choking includes a combination of chest thrusts and back blows. Abdominal thrusts are not used because of their potential for causing injury.
◆ To support the infant during back blows and chest thrusts, place the infant on your arm and support the head and neck while holding the infant's jaw with your thumb and fingers.

51

SKILL PRACTICE: OBSTRUCTED AIRWAY

Time: 40 minutes

Note: *Tell the participants that because the airway obstruction techniques are so similar, it will not be necessary to practice the conscious infant technique. Therefore, there is no skill sheet for Airway Obstruction (Conscious Infant).*

Airway Obstruction (Unconscious Infant)

Activity:

1. Ask the participants to take their skill sheets with them to the practice area.
2. Assign partners or ask participants to find partners.
3. Explain that participants will use a manikin to practice first aid for an unconscious infant whose airway is obstructed.
4. Guide participants through the skill.
5. After participants have practiced the skill to the point at which they feel comfortable in their ability to perform it, have the participants change places. Repeat the practice. Check off participants' skills as you watch them practice.

Lesson 5: BREATHING DEVICES

Length: 1 hour, 20 minutes

Equipment and Supplies:	Video; Skill Sheets: "Using a Resuscitation Mask for Rescue Breathing," "Using a Bag-Valve-Mask Resuscitator for Rescue Breathing (Two-Rescuer)"; Participant Progress Log; adult manikins; decontamination supplies; resuscitation masks; bag-valve masks; blankets or mats
Goal:	Participants will become familiar with the advantages of using the resuscitation mask and the bag-valve-mask resuscitator (BVM) to ventilate a nonbreathing victim.
Knowledge Objectives:	After completing this lesson, participants will be able to—

1. Identify at least three advantages of using breathing devices.
2. Describe how to use a resuscitation mask to ventilate a nonbreathing person.
3. Describe how to use a bag-valve-mask resuscitator to ventilate a nonbreathing person.

Skill Objectives: After completing the class activities, participants will be able to—

1. Demonstrate on a manikin how to use a resuscitation mask to ventilate a nonbreathing person.
2. Demonstrate on a manikin how to use a bag-valve-mask resuscitator to ventilate a nonbreathing person.
3. Make appropriate decisions about care when given an example of an emergency in which a person is not breathing.

RESUSCITATION MASK

Time: 10 minutes

Primary Points:

- Two advantages of the resuscitation mask:
  1. It can be used on breathing and nonbreathing victims.
  2. It reduces the possibility of disease transmission by providing a barrier between the rescuer and the victim.
- Masks should meet certain criteria to be most effective. They should—
  - Be made of transparent, pliable material that allows you to make a tight seal.
  - Have a one-way valve for releasing exhaled air.
  - Have a standard 15mm or 22mm coupling assembly.
  - Have an inlet for the delivery of supplemental oxygen.

53

◆ Work well under a variety of environmental conditions.
◆ Be easy to assemble and use.

Video: Show the video segment: *Using a Resuscitation Mask.*

Primary Points: ◆ Using the mask is a simple skill. Place the mask on the victim's face and—
   ◆ Tilt the head back.
   ◆ Lift the jaw.
   ◆ Open the mouth.

SKILL PRACTICE: RESUSCITATION MASK

Time: 30 minutes

Activity:
1. Ask participants to take skill sheets with them to the practice area.
2. Assign partners or ask participants to find partners.
3. Using manikins, have participants begin with the primary survey. When participants get to the "Check Breathing" step, tell them the victim is not breathing.

Note: Participants should apply the mask and give two breaths, check for a pulse and breathing, then provide rescue breathing through the resuscitation mask.

4. Watch as participants practice, focusing on four steps:
   ◆ Tilting the victim's head back
   ◆ Lifting the jaw with both hands
   ◆ Keeping the mouth open with the thumbs
   ◆ Ventilating only until the chest rises

5. After participants have practiced to the point at which they feel comfortable in their ability to perform rescue breathing with the resuscitation mask, have participants change places. Repeat the practice. Check off participants' skills as you watch them.
6. Answer any questions.

BAG-VALVE-MASK RESUSCITATOR (BVM)

Time: 10 minutes

Primary Points:
- There may be times when you have to use a bag-valve mask (BVM) or are asked to assist with one.
- The bag has three pieces:
  - Self-inflating bag
  - One-way valve
  - The mask, which is very similar to the resuscitation mask
- Using the mask reduces the possibility of disease transmission.
- The BVM delivers 21 percent oxygen (the surrounding air).

Note: *Only when a BVM is used in conjunction with supplemental oxygen is a reservoir attached to the bag.*

- Because it is difficult for one person to maintain a proper seal and head position, using the BVM is recommended as a two-rescuer skill. One rescuer holds the mask in place; the other squeezes the air from the bag into the victim's lungs.

Video: Show the video segment: *Using a Bag-Valve Mask.*

SKILL PRACTICE: BAG-VALVE MASK

Time: 30 minutes

Activity:
1. Ask participants to take skill sheets with them to the practice area.
2. Assign partners or ask participants to find partners.
3. Using manikins, have participants begin with the primary survey. When participants get to the "Check Breathing" step, tell them the victim is not breathing.

Note: *Participants should give two breaths using the BVM; check for a pulse and breathing; then continue ventilations using the BVM.*

4. Watch as participants practice, focusing on four steps:
   - Tilting the victim's head back
   - Lifting the jaw with both hands
   - Keeping the mouth open with the thumbs
   - Ventilating slowly, only until the chest rises

5. After participants have practiced to the point at which they feel comfortable in their ability to ventilate with the BVM, have participants change places. Repeat the practice. Check off participants' skills as you watch them.
6. Answer any questions.

Lesson 6:
CARDIAC EMERGENCIES

Length: 2 hours, 45 minutes

Equipment and Supplies: Video; Skill Sheets: "CPR for an Adult," "CPR for a Child," "CPR for an Infant," "Two-Rescuer CPR—Beginning Together," "Two-Rescuer CPR—Changing Positions"; Participant Progress Log; adult, child, and infant manikins; decontamination supplies; blankets or mats

Goal: Participants will become familiar with the signs and symptoms of a heart attack/cardiac arrest, how to care for victims who experience them, and how to identify and reduce risk factors for cardiovascular disease.

Knowledge Objectives: After completing this lesson, participants will be able to—
1. List at least four signs and symptoms of a heart attack.
2. Describe how to care for a heart attack victim.
3. Identify the primary sign of cardiac arrest.
4. Describe the purpose of CPR.
5. Describe how to give CPR to an adult, a child, and an infant.
6. List the conditions under which a rescuer may stop CPR.
7. Identify risk factors for cardiovascular disease that can be controlled.

Skill Objectives: After completing the class activities, participants will be able to—
1. Demonstrate how to give CPR to an adult, a child, and an infant.
2. Make appropriate decisions about care when given an example of an emergency in which a person is in cardiac arrest.

RECOGNIZING A HEART ATTACK

Time: 15 minutes

Activity:
1. Remind participants that when the heart is deprived of oxygen, heart muscle in the affected area dies. The result may be a heart attack.
2. Tell participants that they are now going to view a video on heart attack. Tell them to note carefully the signs and symptoms of heart attack and the care provided.

57

Video: Show the video segment: *Recognizing a Heart Attack.*

Note: Point out to participants that when the woman calls 9–1–1, she does not give the location of the building. This is because the number is "enhanced" 9–1–1. The location of the call is automatically registered on the dispatcher's computer and appears on the screen.

Primary Points:
- Signs and symptoms of a heart attack:
  - Persistent chest pain
  - Nausea
  - Sweating
  - Looking and feeling ill
  - Shortness of breath (breathing difficulty)
- Heart attack is usually the result of cardiovascular disease (CVD)—disease of the heart and blood vessels.
- Cardiovascular disease is the leading cause of death for adults in the United States.
- Certain factors increase a person's chances of developing cardiovascular disease. These are called risk factors. Some risk factors cannot be changed:
  - Men have a higher risk for cardiovascular disease than women.
  - Having a history of cardiovascular disease in your family increases your chances of developing it.
- Many risk factors can be controlled:
  - Do not smoke.
  - Get sufficient exercise.
  - Keep body weight at an appropriate level.
  - Eat a diet low in fats.
  - Be aware of high blood pressure and take steps to control it.
- Participants should review the Healthy Heart IQ in Chapter 7 of their manual to determine how many of these risk factors apply to them.

CARDIAC ARREST

Time: 15 minutes

Primary Points:
- Cardiac arrest is the condition in which the heart stops beating or beats too weakly to circulate blood effectively.
- Cardiac arrest can be caused by cardiovascular disease, drowning, electrocution, suffocation, poisoning, respiratory arrest, and injuries causing severe blood loss.

- A victim in cardiac arrest is unconscious, not breathing, and without a pulse.
- Some cardiac arrests are very sudden. The victim does not show any signs and symptoms of heart attack before the arrest.
- To give the victim a chance of survival, CPR must be started promptly, followed by early defibrillation and early advanced cardiac care.
- Tell participants to read Appendix A, Automated External Defibrillation (AED) in their manual.

Video: Show the video segment: *Adult CPR.*

- Giving ventilations places oxygen in the blood and chest compressions help move the oxygen-rich blood throughout the body.
- CPR is only stopped when—
  - Another trained rescuer takes over.
  - If you are exhausted and unable to continue.
  - If the victim's heart starts beating.
  - If the rescue becomes unsafe.
  - If more advanced personnel order you to discontinue the attempt.

SKILL PRACTICE: ADULT CPR

Time: 40 minutes

Primary Points:
1. Ask participants to take skill sheets with them to the practice area.
2. Assign partners or ask participants to find partners.
3. Using manikins, review locating proper hand position and giving compressions.
4. When participants have mastered these techniques, add giving rescue breaths alternately with sets of compressions.
5. Instruct participants to practice CPR, beginning with the primary survey.
6. After participants have practiced the skills to the point at which they feel comfortable in their ability to perform them, have them change places. Repeat the practice. Check off participants' skills as you watch them practice.
7. Answer any questions.

CHILD CPR

Time: 10 minutes

Primary Points:

- ◆ Unlike adults, children do not often initially suffer a cardiac emergency. Instead, they suffer a respiratory emergency that results in a cardiac emergency.
- ◆ One way to prevent cardiac emergencies in infants and children is to prevent injuries that lead to cardiac emergencies. Another is to make sure that infants and children receive proper medical care. A third is to recognize the early signs of a respiratory emergency. These signs include—
  - ◆ Agitation.
  - ◆ Drowsiness.
  - ◆ Change in skin color (to pale, blue, or gray).
  - ◆ Increased difficulty breathing.
  - ◆ Increased heart and breathing rates.

Video: Show the video segment: *Child CPR.*

SKILL PRACTICE: CHILD CPR

Time: 15 minutes

Activity:

1. Ask participants to take skill sheets with them to the practice area.
2. Assign partners or ask participants to find partners.
3. Guide participants through the skill.
4. After participants have practiced the skill to the point at which they feel comfortable in their ability to perform it, have them change places. Check off participants' skills as you watch them practice.
5. Answer any questions.

INFANT CPR

Time: 10 minutes

Primary Points:

- ◆ The rate of chest compressions for an infant is faster than for an adult or child.
- ◆ Two or three fingers are used to compress the chest.
- ◆ As in child CPR, the rescuer compresses the chest 5 times and ventilates once.

Video: Show the video segment: *Infant CPR.*

SKILL PRACTICE: INFANT CPR

Time: 15 minutes

Activity:

1. Ask the participants to take skill sheets with them to the practice area.
2. Assign partners or ask participants to find partners.
3. Guide participants through the skill.
4. After participants have practiced the skill to the point at which they feel comfortable in their ability to perform it, have them change places. Check off participants' skills as you watch them practice.
5. Answer any questions.

TWO-RESCUER CPR

Time: 10 minutes

Video:

Show the video: *Two-Rescuer CPR.*

Primary Points:

- In two-rescuer CPR, the ratio of compressions to breaths is 5 to 1.
- When two rescuers begin CPR together, the first rescuer does a primary survey and the second rescuer gets into position to give chest compressions.
- When CPR is in progress by one rescuer and a second rescuer arrives, that rescuer should ask whether advanced medical personnel have been summoned. If they have, the second rescuer can then assist the first rescuer in giving two-rescuer CPR.
  - This can be done without interrupting the flow of CPR. The second rescuer enters immediately after the first rescuer has completed a cycle of 15 compressions and 2 breaths.
  - The second rescuer gets into position at the chest and finds the correct hand position. The first rescuer checks the pulse. If there is no pulse, the second rescuer begins compressions.
- If a rescuer becomes tired, he or she can change positions with the other rescuer. When the rescuers change, the rescuer at the victim's head completes 1 breath and then moves to the chest. The rescuer at the chest completes 5 compressions and then moves to the head. Both rescuers move quickly into position without changing sides.

SKILL PRACTICE: TWO-RESCUER CPR

Time: 35 minutes

Activity:

1. Ask participants to take skill sheets with them to the practice area.
2. Assign partners or ask participants to find partners.
3. Guide participants through two rescuers beginning CPR together.
4. After participants have practiced the skill to the point at which they feel comfortable in their ability to perform it, have them change places. Check off participants' skills as you watch them practice.
5. When participants have mastered these techniques, review two rescuers changing positions.
6. Have participants practice this skill until they are comfortable in performing it. Check off participants' skills as you watch them practice.
7. Answer any questions.

Lesson 7:
SPECIAL RESUSCITATION SITUATIONS

20 minutes

Equipment and Supplies: None

Goal: Participants will become familiar with four special situations requiring modification of emergency care procedures and with the care to give for them.

Knowledge Objectives: After completing this lesson, participants will be able to—

1. Identify four special situations that require modifying emergency care procedures.
2. Describe the procedures for giving emergency care to victims of—
   - Near drowning.
   - Electric shock and lightning strike.
   - Traumatic injury.
   - Hypothermia.
3. Describe the guidelines for performing CPR in difficult situations or locations.

Activity:

Introduction

1. Tell participants that certain situations require the professional rescuer to modify the care he or she normally uses. The most common special situations are—
   - Near drowning.
   - Electric shock and lightning strike.
   - Traumatic injury.
   - Hypothermia.

   They will also need to learn what to do if they need to give CPR in certain difficult locations and situations.

NEAR DROWNING

Time: 5 minutes

Primary Points:
- A person who has been submerged for more than 2 or 3 minutes will suffer from lack of oxygen and need emergency care.
- A rescuer should get to the victim as soon as possible without risking personal safety.
- Use something that floats—a life preserver, rescue tube, ring buoy, surfboard, raft, and so on—to help in the rescue.

♦ If you suspect head or spine injury, support the victim's head and neck and float the victim onto a backboard or surfboard before removing from the water. If you need to turn the victim, support the head, neck, and trunk and turn as a unit. Give rescue breathing without tilting the victim's head.

♦ Check airway, breathing, and circulation. Provide care based on the victim's condition. If you are unable to adequately ventilate the victim, do the Heimlich maneuver to clear any obstruction and continue your attempts to ventilate.

♦ Regardless of speed of recovery, every near-drowning victim needs follow-up care at a medical facility.

ELECTRIC SHOCK, LIGHTNING STRIKE, AND TRAUMATIC INJURY

Time: 5 minutes

Electric Shock

Primary Points:

♦ Electric shock causes between 500 and 1,000 deaths each year in the United States. An additional 5,000 people receive emergency treatment. Electric shock can cause serious burns and also paralyze the breathing muscles, causing cardiac arrest.

♦ The severity of an electric shock is affected by—
  ♦ Duration of contact with the source of the electricity.
  ♦ Strength of the current.
  ♦ Environmental conditions.

♦ Immediately after a severe shock, the victim may not be breathing and may be without a pulse.

♦ Never approach the victim until the source of the electricity is turned off.

♦ As soon as it is safe, check the victim's airway, breathing, and pulse. Start rescue breathing or CPR at once if necessary.

Lightning

Primary Points:

♦ Lightning acts as a direct current that interrupts the heart's rhythm.

♦ Victims who suffer immediate cardiac arrest are those most likely to die.

♦ Victims can be resuscitated even if some time has passed before attempts are made.

♦ Lightning strike can cause severe fractures, including spinal fracture, and severe burns.

Traumatic Injury

Primary Points:

- ◆ Survival rates from cardiac arrest as the result of trauma are extremely poor.
- ◆ The victim must be transported as soon as possible to a trauma center, where he or she will receive specialized treatment.
- ◆ Suspect head or spine injury in a trauma victim, especially a victim of a fall from a height, a motor vehicle accident, or a diving or skiing accident. Be sure the head and neck are stabilized before you open the airway.

HYPOTHERMIA

Time: 5 minutes

Primary Points:

- ◆ In hypothermia, the entire body cools and body temperature drops below 95° Fahrenheit (35° C). In severe hypothermia, body temperature is below 86° Fahrenheit (30° C).
- ◆ The victim will die if not given care.
- ◆ A growing concern in the United States is the number of people dying each year from cold exposure. These fatalities are associated with the increasing number of homeless and older adults.
- ◆ Signs and symptoms of hypothermia include—
  - ◆ Shivering.
  - ◆ Numbness.
  - ◆ Apathy.
  - ◆ Decreasing level of consciousness.
  - ◆ Erratic heartbeat.
  - ◆ Rigid muscles.
- ◆ If the victim is not breathing, begin rescue breathing. The pulse may be hard to find, so check the victim's pulse for at least 45 seconds and as long as one minute. If the victim has no pulse, begin CPR.
- ◆ The victim should be transported to a medical facility at once and should continue to be given CPR on the way.
- ◆ Prevent further heat loss by removing any wet clothing and protecting the victim from wind or cold.
- ◆ Warm the body gradually by wrapping the victim in blankets or dry clothing.
- ◆ Handle the victim gently. Rough handling and rapid rewarming can cause dangerous heart rhythms.

CPR IN DIFFICULT SITUATIONS AND LOCATIONS

Time: 5 minutes

Activity:

- ◆ Use the following guidelines if you find yourself having to perform CPR in certain situations.
  - ◆ Only move a victim from a cramped or busy location if it is unsafe or impractical to perform CPR.
  - ◆ If a victim has to be transported up or down a flight of stairs, perform CPR at the head or foot of the stairs. Then, using a predetermined signal, interrupt CPR, move quickly to the next level, and resume CPR. Try not to interrupt CPR for more than 30 seconds.
  - ◆ Do not interrupt CPR while a victim is being transferred to an ambulance or into the emergency department. With a high litter or bed, you may have to kneel beside the victim on the bed or litter or stand on a stool next to the bed or litter rails to get sufficient height to adequately compress the chest.

Lesson 8:
WRITTEN EXAMINATION

45 minutes

Equipment and Supplies: Copies of exams A and B and answer sheets for each participant; pencils

Activity:

1. Tell participants that they will now take a 50-question examination. They will have 40 minutes to complete the exam and must answer at least 40 questions correctly to pass. They may not use their textbooks to find the answers.
2. Hand out an examination and answer sheet to each participant.
3. Tell participants to write only on the answer sheet, mark answers clearly, and use pencil only in case they want to erase or change an answer.
4. Tell them to check their answers before handing them in.
5. Tell them to come to you or raise one hand when they have finished the exam or have any questions.
6. Score the exams. The answer keys for both exams are at the end of the manual.

Note: As participants hand in their answer sheets and exams, quickly grade each exam and return it to the correct participant so he or she can review any missed questions. If time allows, discuss with the class any exam items that were a problem. Collect all answer sheets and exams before the participants leave the class. If a participant fails the exam, ask him or her to see you after class to schedule a retest.

7. Give a copy of the Course Evaluation form (Appendix C) to each participant as he or she completes the written exam. Ask participants to leave the evaluations in a box or envelope you have provided near the door.
8. Thank all participants for attending the course.

Part C: Appendixes

Appendix A

Recommendations on Manikin Decontamination

Excerpted from "Standards and Guidelines for Cardiopulmonary Resuscitation and Emergency Cardiac Care," Journal of the American Medical Association, No. 16 (October 28, 1992); 268;2195–2197. Copyright 1993, American Medical Association. Used with permission.

SAFETY DURING CPR TRAINING AND ACTUAL RESCUE

Safety during CPR training and in actual rescue situations in which CPR is provided has gained increased attention. This section addresses both these issues. Adherence to the following recommendations should minimize possible complications for instructors and students during CPR training and implementation. The recommendations for manikin decontamination and rescuer safety originally established in 1978 by the Centers for Disease Control[1] were updated in 1983 and again in 1989 by the AHA, the American Red Cross, and the Centers for Disease Control to minimize possible complications during CPR training and in actual emergencies.[2,3]

Disease Transmission During CPR Training
The 1980s brought about a dramatic increase in inquiries about the possible role of CPR training manikins in transmitting diseases such as human immunodeficiency virus (HIV), hepatitis B virus (HBV), herpes viruses, and various upper and lower respiratory infections such as influenza, infectious mononucleosis, and tuberculosis. It is estimated that approximately 70 million people in the United States have had direct contact with manikins during CPR training courses. Use of these manikins has never been documented as being responsible for an outbreak or even an isolated case of bacterial, fungal, or viral disease.[4]

However, under certain circumstances manikin surfaces present a remote risk of disease transmission. Therefore, manikin surfaces should be cleaned and disinfected in a consistent way.

There are two important infection control considerations in CPR training. First, practice on manikins can result in contamination from trainee hands or oral secretions. If manikins are not cleaned properly between each use and after each class, these contaminants may be transmitted. Second, internal parts such as the valve mechanisms and artificial lungs in manikin airways invariably become contaminated during use. If not dismantled and cleaned or replaced after class, they may become sources of contamination for subsequent classes. There is no evidence, however, that manikin valve mechanisms produce aerosols even

71

when air is forcibly expelled during chest compression. In addition, a number of manufacturers produce different types of manikins for training purposes. Since these manikins have unique features, instructors and training agencies rely heavily on the manufacturers' recommendations for manikin use and maintenance, which should be carefully followed.

Neither HBV nor HIV is as resistant to disinfectant chemicals as previously thought.[5-7] Studies have shown that the retroviral agent that causes acquired immune deficiency syndrome (AIDS), HIV, is comparatively delicate and is inactivated in less than 10 minutes at room temperature by a number of disinfectants, including those agents recommended for manikin cleaning.[8-9] It is emphasized that there is no evidence to date that HIV/AIDS is transmitted by casual personal contact, indirect contact with inanimate surfaces, or the airborne route. The recommendations that follow adequately protect against transmission of either virus, as well as bacterial and fungal infections.

Recommendations
The following recommendations should be adhered to when conducting CPR training courses:

1. Purchasers of training manikins should thoroughly follow the manufacturer's recommendations and provisions for sanitary practice. These recommendations generally have FDA review and approval.

2. Students should be told in advance that training sessions will involve close physical contact with manikins used by their fellow students.

3. Students or instructors should postpone CPR training if they are known to be in the active stages of an infectious disease, have reason to believe they have been exposed to an infectious disease, or have dermatologic lesions on their hands, mouths, or circumoral areas.

4. Chronic infections such as HBV and HIV persist over an extended period and can be transmitted even when the carrier is asymptomatic. If an instructor wishes to train someone with a known chronic infection or if the instructor has a known chronic infection, precautions should be taken to protect other participants from exposure. This is best accomplished by providing the infected person with a separate manikin not used by anyone else until it has been cleaned according to recommended end-of-class decontamination procedures. Requests for individual manikins should be honored, within reason. Equitable accommodations for all participants are encouraged. In such instances the infected person should have his or her personal physician review the circumstances carefully and indicate whether participation is appropriate.

5. If more than one CPR manikin is used in a particular training class, students should preferably be assigned in pairs, with each pair having contact with only one manikin. This would lessen the possible contamination of several manikins by one person, therefore limiting possible exposure of other class members.

6. Instructors in CPR should practice good hygiene by washing their hands before handling manikins and avoiding eating during class. Procedures for cleaning and maintaining manikins and accessories (e.g., face shields and resuscitation masks) should also be practiced. Manikins should be inspected routinely for signs of physical deterioration, such as cracks or tears in plastic surfaces, which make careful cleaning difficult or impossible. The manikins' hair or clothing should be washed periodically (perhaps monthly or if obviously soiled).

7. During two-rescuer CPR training, there is no opportunity to disinfect the manikin between students when the switching procedure is practiced. To limit the potential for disease transmission during this exercise, the second student taking over ventilation on the manikin should simulate ventilation instead of blowing into the manikin.

8. During training in the obstructed airway procedure, the student uses his or her finger to sweep matter out of the manikin's mouth. This action could contaminate the student's finger with exhaled moisture and saliva from previous students or contaminate the manikin with material from the student's finger. When practicing this procedure, the finger sweep should either be simulated or done on a manikin whose airway was decontaminated before the procedure and will be decontaminated after the procedure.

9. Manikins should be cleaned as soon as possible at the end of each class to avoid drying of contaminants on manikin surfaces. Personnel disassembling and decontaminating the manikins should wear protective latex gloves and wash their hands when finished. Disassemble the manikins as directed by the manufacturer. As indicated, thoroughly wash all external and internal surfaces as well as reusable protective face shields with warm soapy water and brushes. Rinse all surfaces with fresh water. Wet all surfaces with a sodium hypochlorite solution of at least 500 ppm free available chlorine (1/4 cup liquid household bleach per gallon of tap water) for 10 minutes. This solution must be made fresh for each class and discarded after each use. Rinse with fresh water and immediately dry all external and internal surfaces. Rinsing with alcohol will aid drying of internal surfaces, which will prevent the survival and growth of bacterial or fungal pathogens if the manikins are stored for periods longer than the day of cleaning.

10. If used, the individual protective face shield should be changed each time a different student uses the manikin in a training class. Between use by students and after demonstrations by the instructor, the manikin's face and the inside of its mouth should be wiped vigorously. Use a clean, absorbent material (e.g., 4 x 4 inch gauze pad) wet with either the hypochlorite solution described above or with 70% alcohol (isopropanol or ethanol). The surfaces should remain wet for at least 30 seconds before they are wiped dry with a second piece of clean, absorbent material.

The use of alcohols is recommended in this instance as an alternative, since some persons object to the odor of sodium hypochlorite. Although highly bactericidal, alcohols are not considered broad-spectrum agents, and use of alcohols here is recommended primarily as an aid in mechanical cleaning. In a short contact period, alcohols may not be as effective against pathogens, but in the context of vigorous cleaning with alcohol and absorbent material, little viable microbial contamination of any kind is likely after cleaning.

11. Instructors in CPR should be encouraged not to rely solely on the use of a disinfectant to protect themselves and their students from cross-infection during training. Thorough physical cleaning (scrubbing and wiping) should be emphasized as the first step in an effective decontamination protocol. Microbial contamination is easily removed from smooth, nonporous surfaces with disposable cleaning cloths moistened with a detergent solution. There is no evidence that soaking alone is as effective as soaking accompanied by vigorous scrubbing.

If these recommendations are consistently followed, students in each class should be able to use manikins whose cleanliness equals or exceeds that of properly cleaned eating utensils. A higher level of surface disinfection is not warranted, and the recommended disinfectant chemicals (household bleach or alcohol) are safe, effective, inexpensive, easily obtained, and well tolerated by students, instructors, and manikin surfaces when used properly.

The risk of transmission of any infectious disease by manikin practice appears to be very low. Although millions of people worldwide have used training manikins in the last 25 years, there has never been a documented case of transmission of bacterial, fungal, or viral disease by a CPR training manikin. Thus, in the absence of evidence of infectious disease transmission, the lifesaving potential of CPR should continue to be vigorously emphasized and energetic efforts in support of broad-scale CPR training should be continued.

Disease Transmission During Actual Performance of CPR

The vast majority of CPR performed in the United States is done by health care and public safety personnel, many of whom assist in ventilation of respiratory and cardiac arrest victims about whom they have little or no medical information. A layperson is far less likely to perform CPR than health care providers. The layperson who performs CPR, whether on an adult or pediatric victim, is most likely to do so in the home, where 70% to 80% of respiratory and cardiac arrests occur.[10]

The layperson who responds to an emergency in an unknown victim should be guided by individual moral and ethical values and knowledge of risks that may exist in various rescue situations. It is safest for the rescuer to assume that any emergency situation that involves exposure to certain body fluids has the potential for disease transmission for both the rescuer and victim.

The greatest concern over the risk of disease transmission should be directed to persons who perform CPR frequently, such as health care providers, both in the hospital and in the prehospital environment. Providers of prehospital emergency health care include paramedics, EMTs, law enforcement personnel, firefighters, lifeguards, and others whose job-defined duties require them to perform first-response medical care. The risk of disease transmission from infected persons to providers of prehospital emergency health care should be no higher than that for those providing emergency care in the hospital if appropriate precautions are taken to prevent exposure to blood or other body fluids.

The probability that a rescuer (lay or professional) will become infected with HBV or HIV as a result of performing CPR is minimal.[11] Although transmission of HBV and HIV between health care workers and patients has been documented as a result of blood exchange or penetration of the skin by blood-contaminated instruments,[12] to date, transmission of HBV and HIV infection during mouth-to-mouth resuscitation has not been documented.[13]

Direct mouth-to-mouth resuscitation will likely result in exchange of saliva between the victim and rescuer. However, HBV-positive saliva has not been shown to be infectious even to oral mucous membranes, through contamination of shared musical instruments, or through HBV carriers.[14] In addition, saliva has not been implicated in the transmission of HIV after bites, percutaneous inoculation, or contamination of cuts and open wounds with saliva from HIV-infected patients.[15] The theoretical risk of infection is greater for salivary or aerosol transmission of herpes simplex, *Neisseria meningitides*, and airborne diseases such as tuberculosis and other respiratory infections. Rare instances of herpes transmission during CPR have been reported.[16]

The emergence of multidrug-resistant tuberculosis[17–18] and the risk of tuberculosis to emergency workers[19] is a cause for concern. In most instances, transmission of tuberculosis requires prolonged close exposure as is likely to occur in households, but transmission to emergency workers can occur during resuscitative efforts by either the airborne route[20] or by direct contact. The magnitude of the risk is uncertain but probably low.

After performing mouth-to-mouth resuscitation on a person suspected of having tuberculosis, the caregiver should be evaluated for tuberculosis using standard approaches based on the caregiver's baseline skin tests.[21] Caregivers with negative baseline skin tests should be retested 12 weeks later.

Preventive therapy should be considered for all persons with positive tests and should be started on all converters.[22] In areas where multidrug-resistant tuberculosis is common or after exposure to known multidrug-resistant tuberculosis, the choice of preventive therapeutic agent is uncertain, but some authorities suggest two or more agents.[23]

Performance of mouth-to-mouth resuscitation or invasive procedures can result in the exchange of blood between the victim and rescuer. This is especially true in cases of trauma or if either victim or rescuer has breaks in the skin on or around the lips or soft tissues of the oral cavity mucosa. Thus, a theoretical risk of HBV and HIV transmission during mouth-to-mouth resuscitation exists.

Because of the concern about disease transmission between victim and rescuer, rescuers with a duty to provide CPR should follow the precautions and guidelines established by the Centers for Disease Control[24] and the Occupational Safety and Health Administration. These guidelines include the use of barriers, such as latex gloves, and mechanical ventilation equipment, such as bag-valve mask and other resuscitation masks with valves capable of diverting expired air from the rescuer. Rescuers who have an infection that may be transmitted by blood or saliva should not perform mouth-to-mouth resuscitation if circumstances allow other immediate or effective methods of ventilation.

The perceived risk of disease transmission during CPR has reduced the willingness of some laypersons to initiate mouth-to-mouth ventilation in unknown victims of cardiac arrest. Public education is vital to alleviate this fear. In addition, if such concern is identified, rescuers should be encouraged to learn mouth-to-mouth barrier device (face mask or face shield) ventilation. If a lone rescuer refuses to initiate mouth-to-mouth ventilation, he or she should at least access the EMS system, open the airway, and perform chest compressions until a rescuer arrives who is willing to provide ventilation or until ventilation can be initiated by skilled rescuers (arriving EMT/paramedics) with the necessary barrier devices.

Although the efficacy of barrier devices has not been documented conclusively, those with a duty to respond should be instructed during CPR training in the use of masks with one-way valves. Plastic mouth and nose covers with filtered openings are also available and may provide a degree of protection.[25] Masks without one-way valves (including those with S-shaped devices) offer little, if any, protection and should not be considered for routine use. Since intubation obviates the need for mouth-to-mouth resuscitation and is more effective than the use of masks alone, early intubation is encouraged when equipment and trained professionals are available. Resuscitation equipment known or suspected to be contaminated with blood or other body fluids should be discarded or thoroughly cleaned and disinfected after each use.[26] Following these precautions and guidelines should further reduce the risk of disease transmission when providing CPR.

References

1. *Recommendations for Decontaminating Manikins Used in Cardiopulmonary Resuscitation: Hepatitis Surveillance*, Report 42. Atlanta, GA: Centers for Disease Control; 1978;34–36.

2. Standards and guidelines for cardiopulmonary resuscitation (CPR) and emergency cardiac care (ECC). *JAMA*. 1986;255:2905–2989.

3. The Emergency Cardiac Care Committee of the American Heart Association: Risk of infection during CPR training and rescue: supplemental guidelines. *JAMA*. 1989;262:2714–2715.

4. Ibid, fn 3.

5. Favero MS, Bond WW. Sterilization, disinfection and antisepsis in the hospital. In: Balows A, Hausler WJ Jr, Hermann KL, Eisenberg HD, Shadom HJ, eds. *Manual of Clinical Microbiology*. 5th ed. Washington, DC: American Society for Microbiology; 1991;183–200.

6. Centers for Disease Control. Acquired immune deficiency syndrome (AIDS); precautions for clinical and laboratory staffs. *MMWR*. 1982;31:577–580.

7. A hospital-wide approach to AIDS: recommendations of the Advisory Committee on Infections within Hospitals. American Hospital Association. *Infect Control*. 1984;5:242–248.

8. Resnik LK, Veren K, Salahuddin SF, Tondreau S, Markham PD. Stability and inactivation of HTLV-III/LAV under clinical and laboratory environments. *JAMA*. 1986;255:1187–1191.

9. Spire B, Dormont D, Barre Sinoussi F, Montagnier L, Chermann JC. In activation of lymphadenopathy-associated with heat, gamma rays, and ultraviolet light. *Lancet*. 1985;1:188–189.

10. Ibid, fn. 2.

11. Centers for Disease Control. Guidelines for prevention of transmission of human immunodeficiency virus and hepatitis B virus to health care and public safety workers. *MMWR.* 1989;38(suppl 6):1–37.

12. Marcus R. Surveillance of health care workers exposed to blood from patients infected with the human immunodeficiency virus. *N Engl J Med.* 1988;319:1118–1123.

13. Sande MA. Transmission of AIDS: the case against casual contagion. *N Engl J Med.* 1986;314:380–382.

14. Ibid, fn. 11.

15. Friedland GH, Saltzman BR, Rogers MF, et al. Lack of transmission of HTLV-III/LAV infection to household contacts of patients with AIDS or AIDS-related complex with oral candidiasis. *N Engl J Med.* 1986;314:344–349.

16. Hendricks AA, Shapiro EP. Primary herpes simplex infection following mouth-to-mouth resuscitation. *JAMA* 1980;243:257–258.

17. Centers for Disease Control. Outbreak of multidrug-resistant-tuberculosis—Texas, California, and Pennsylvania. *MMWR.* 1990;39:369–372.

18. Centers for Disease Control. Nosocomial transmission of multidrug-resistant tuberculosis among HIV-infected persons—Florida and New York, 1988–1991. *MMWR.* 1991;40:585–591.

19. Haley CE, McDonald RC, Rossi L, Jones WD Jr, Haley RW, Luby JP. Tuberculosis epidemic among hospital personnel. *Infect Control Hosp Epidemiol.* 1989;10:204–210.

20. Ibid, fn. 19.

21. Dooley SW Jr, Castro KG, Hutton MD, Mullan RJ, Polder JA, Snider DE Jr. Guidelines for preventing the transmission of tuberculosis in health-care settings with special focus on HIV-related issues. *MMWR.* 1990;39:1–29.

22. Centers for Disease Control. The use of preventive therapy for tuberculosis infection in the United States: recommendation of the Advisory Committee for Elimination of Tuberculosis. *MMWR.* 1990;39:9–12.

23. Steinberg JL, Nardell EA, Kass EH. Antibiotic prophylaxis after exposure to antibiotic-resistant Mycobacterium tuberculosis. *Rev Infect Dis.* 1988;10:1208–1219.

24. Ibid, fn. 11.

25. Recommendation for prevention of HIV transmission in healthcare settings. *MMWR.* 1987;36(No. 25):1S–18S.

26. Ibid, fn. 25.

Risk of Infection During CPR Training and Rescue: Supplemental Guidelines

The American Heart Association and the American Red Cross used the findings from the 1985 National Conference on Standards and Guidelines for Cardiopulmonary Resuscitation and Emergency Cardiac Care to establish their policy on the risk of infection during cardiopulmonary resuscitation (CPR) training and rescue. Findings that support the safety of CPR training and rescue and appropriate risk reduction strategies are presented as an update to the 1985 article. The Emergency Cardiac Care Committee of the American Heart Association incorporated recent advisories from the Centers for Disease Control as well as other information into guidelines that augment earlier recommendations.

(JAMA. 1989;262:2714–2715)

FINDINGS from the 1985 National Conference on Standards and Guidelines for Cardiopulmonary Resuscitation and Emergency Cardiac Care are the basis of the official position of both the American Heart Association and the American Red Cross on risk of infections during cardiopulmonary resuscitation (CPR) training and rescue. These guidelines[1] have been augmented by advisories from the Centers for Disease Control released in 1987[2] and 1988[3] and from the National Institute of Occupational Safety and Health in 1989.[4]

The Emergency Cardiac Care Committee of the American Heart Association considered specific issues related to risk of infection associated with both training and on-site rescue. The American Heart Association and the American Red Cross recommend the following guidelines for adoption.

GUIDELINES FOR RESCUERS WITH KNOWN OR SUSPECTED INFECTIONS

Transmission of hepatitis B virus (HBV) between health care workers and patients has been documented. Instruments and patients' open wounds have been contaminated when health care workers with high concentrations of HBV (much higher than that achieved in human immunodeficiency virus [HIV] infections) in their blood sustained a puncture wound while performing invasive procedures or had weeping lesions or small lacerations on their hands. Transmission of HIV from patients to health care workers has been documented in cases of blood exchange or penetration of the skin by blood-contaminated instruments.[5]

Direct mouth-to-mouth resuscitation will likely result in exchange of saliva between victim and rescuer. Hepatitis B-positive saliva has not been shown to be infectious, however, when applied to oral mucous membranes or through contamination of shared musical instruments or CPR training mannequins used by hepatitis B carriers. In addition, saliva has not been implicated in the transmission of HIV after bites, percutaneous inoculation, or contamination of cuts and open wounds with saliva from HIV-infected patients.[6-7]

Performance of mouth-to-mouth resuscitation or invasive procedures can result in exchange of blood between victim and rescuer if either has had breaks in the skin on or around the lips or soft tissues of the oral cavity mucosa. Thus, there is a theoretical risk of HBV and HIV transmission during mouth-to-mouth resuscitation.[8] It is important to note that the theoretical risk of infection is greater for salivary or aerosol transmission of herpes simplex and *Neisseria meningitidis* and for transmission of airborne diseases such as tuberculosis and respiratory infections.

• *Regardless of the type of infection, rescuers who have an infection that may be transmitted by blood or saliva or who believe they have been exposed to such an infection should not perform mouth-to-mouth resuscitation if circumstances allow other immediate or effective methods of ventilation, such as use of a bag-valve mask.*

GUIDELINES FOR RESCUERS WITH A DUTY TO PROVIDE CPR

The probability of a rescuer's becoming infected with HBV or HIV as a result of performing CPR is minimal.[4] To date, transmission of HBV or HIV infection during mouth-to-mouth resuscitation has not been documented.[9] However, to minimize the risk of transmitting a variety of diseases, mechanical ventilation or barrier devices should be accessible to those asked to provide CPR in the course of their employment. This includes emergency medical service personnel, firefighters, police, and lifeguards, as well as hospital and clinic health care workers.

Although efficacy in preventing disease transmission has not been demonstrated conclusively, masks with one-way valves and bag-valve devices are available, and those with a duty to respond should be instructed in their use during training. Plastic mouth and nose covers with filtered openings also are available and *may* provide a degree of protection against transfer of oral fluids and aerosols. Masks without one-way valves (including those with S-shaped mouthpieces) and handkerchiefs offer little, if any, protection and should not be considered for routine use. Intubation obviates the need for mouth-to-mouth resuscitation and is more effective than the use of bag-valve-mask devices. Early intubation should be encouraged when equipment and trained professionals are available.

• *Individuals with a duty to respond are reminded of their moral, ethical, and, in certain situations, legal obligations to provide CPR, especially in the occupational setting.*

GUIDELINES FOR THE LAYPERSON

The layperson who responds in an emergency should be guided by individual moral and ethical values and knowledge of risks that may exist in various rescue situations. It is safest for the rescuer to assume that all emergency situations that involve transfer of certain body fluids have the potential for disease transmission for both rescuer and victim.

Intact skin is the primary defense against transmission of blood-borne diseases during CPR. Transmission of HBV or HIV is more likely if the rescuer has lesions, cuts, or sores in or around the mouth or on the hands and has contact with the victim's blood, vomitus that contains blood, and/or saliva that contains blood. A rescuer who believes he or she has had parenteral or mucous membrane contact with the victim's blood or blood-contaminated body fluids should wash promptly and thoroughly and contact a physician.

• *As a minimum action, in situations perceived as high-risk for disease transmission, the lay rescuer should assess the victim's responsiveness, call for help, position the victim, open the airway, and, in the absence of a pulse, perform chest compressions.*[10] *However, the rescuer should remember that delayed ventilation could mean death or disablement for an otherwise healthy person, while risk to the rescuer, even with a known HBV/HIV-positive victim, is considered very low.*

CPR TRAINING FOR INFECTED INDIVIDUALS

To date, transmission of HBV infection through use of CPR mannequins by HBV carriers has not been shown. Neither has saliva been implicated in HIV transmission. Because of potential breakdown of oral and circumoral mucosa during practice on a mannequin, however, CPR training poses a theoretical risk to class participants. It is recommended that students and instructors adhere to the guidelines that follow.

Acute Infections or Dermatologic Lesions

Acute respiratory infections such as the common cold run a short course, and most breaks in the skin heal naturally or after medical attention. Therefore, students and instructors should postpone CPR training if they (1) are known to be in the active stage of an infection, (2) have reason to believe they have been exposed to an infectious disease, or (3) have dermatologic lesions on their hands or in oral or circumoral areas.

Chronic Infections

Chronic infections such as HBV and HIV persist over an extended period and can be transmitted even when the carrier is asymptomatic. If an instructor wishes to train or to present course completion cards to an individual with a known chronic infection or if the instructor has a known chronic infection, precautions must be taken to protect other participants from exposure. This is best accomplished by providing the infected individual with a separate mannequin that is not used by anyone else until it has been cleaned according to recommended end-of-class decontamination procedures.

• *An individual who has an acute or chronic infection that may be transmitted by blood or saliva must not participate in CPR training until his or her personal physician has reviewed the circumstances carefully and indicated whether participation is appropriate. Because CPR course participants may not know that they have been exposed to an infection, it is imperative that participants and instructors adhere strictly to established procedures for decontamination of the mannequin.*[11] *In addition, requests for individual mannequins should be honored, within reason. Equitable accommodations for all participants in CPR programs are encouraged.*

EDUCATION FOR THE CHRONICALLY INFECTED RESCUER

Individuals with chronic infections should be educated about potential transmission of infection to victims during CPR. Course participants should be made aware of guidelines for rescuers with known or suspected infections. Health risks to the chronically infected rescuer also should be emphasized. If the rescuer's immune system has been altered by any cause, performance of CPR may pose a greater risk to the rescuer. Contact with a victim who is in the active stage of an infection (e.g., influenza, tuberculosis, HBV infection, and other respiratory infections) may jeopardize the health of the rescuer with depressed immune function.

GUIDELINES FOR INDIVIDUALS UNABLE TO COMPLETE A CPR COURSE

It is the position of the American Heart Association and the American Red Cross that all reasonable accommodations should be made to provide CPR training to anyone who desires it. It is understood, however, that not everyone will be able to meet the standards required for completion of a CPR course. Such individuals include, but are not limited to, those with physical disabilities that prevent acute ventilation of a mannequin or patient, those unable to perform adequate chest compressions, and those with chronic infections. This may create a dilemma for an individual whose job requires CPR course completion.

Whether an infected worker can care for patients adequately and safely must be determined on an individual basis. The worker's personal physician should make this decision in conjunction with the employing agency and its medical advisers.

• *It is not the role of the American Heart Association or the American Red Cross to lower their course completion standards to accommodate, for purposes of employment, individuals unable to meet these standards. This is an issue that must be resolved by the employer and the employee; thus, the employer must decide whether to waive the CPR course completion requirement. The more important issue for someone who is unable to complete the desired course is whether he or she is able to work in a situation that requires administration of CPR.*

Approved by the Steering Committee of the American Heart Association.

References

1. Standards and guidelines for cardiopulmonary resuscitation and emergency cardiac care. *JAMA.* 1986;255:2905–3044.
2. Centers for Disease Control. Recommendations for prevention of HIV transmission in health-care settings. *MMWR.* 1987;36 (suppl 2):1S–18S.
3. Centers for Disease Control. Update: universal precautions for prevention of transmission of human immunodeficiency virus, hepatitis B virus, and other bloodborne pathogens in health-care settings. *MMWR.* 1988;37:377–382, 387–388.
4. Centers for Disease Control. Guidelines for prevention of transmission of human immunodeficiency virus and hepatitis B virus to health-care and public safety workers. *MMWR.* 1989;38(suppl 6):1–37.

5. Marcus R, the CDC Cooperative Needlestick Surveillance Group. Surveillance of health care workers exposed to blood from patients infected with human immunodeficiency virus. *N Engl J Med*. 1988;319:1118–1123.

6. Fox PC, Wolff A, Yeh CK, Atkinson JC, Baum BJ. Saliva inhibits HIV-1 infectivity. *J Am Dent Assoc*. 1988;116:635–637.

7. Friedland GH, Saltzman BR, Rogers MF, Lesser ML, Mayers MM, Klein RS. Lack of transmission of HTLV III/LAV infection to household contacts of patients with AIDS or AIDS-related complex with oral candidiasis. *N Engl J Med*. 1986;314:344–349.

8. Piazza M, Chirianni A, Picciotto L, Guadagnino V, Orlando R, Cataldo PT. Passionate kissing and microlesions of the oral mucosa: possible role in AIDS transmission. *JAMA*. 1989; 261:244–245.

9. Sande MA. Transmission of AIDS: the case against causal contagion. *N Engl J Med*. 1986;314:380–382.

10. Lesser R, Bircher N, Safar P, Stezoski W. Sternal compression before ventilation in cardiopulmonary resuscitation (CPR). *J World Assoc Emerg Disaster Med*. 1985;1(suppl 1):239–241.

11. Centers for Disease Control. *Understanding AIDS: A Message From the Surgeon General*. Washington, DC: US Dept of Health and Human Services; 1988.

Appendix B

Written Exams and Answer Sheet

This appendix contains—
◆ Two 50-item exams—Exam A and Exam B
◆ A blank 50-item answer sheet

You will find two answer keys at the end of the manual.

American Red Cross CPR for the Professional Rescuer Exam A

IMPORTANT: Read all instructions before beginning this exam.

INSTRUCTIONS: Mark all answers in pencil on a separate answer sheet. Do not write on this exam. The questions on this exam are multiple choice. Read each question slowly and carefully. Then choose the **best** answer and fill in that circle on the answer sheet. If you wish to change an answer, erase your first answer completely. Return this exam to your instructor when you are finished.

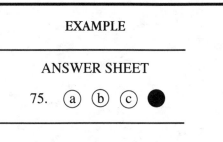

EXAMPLE

ANSWER SHEET

75. ⓐ ⓑ ⓒ ●

75. Why does the American Red Cross teach this course?

    a. To help people stay calm in emergencies

    b. To help people make appropriate decisions when they confront an emergency

    c. To help people in an emergency keep a victim's injuries from getting worse until EMS arrives

    d. All of the above

1. Which person in the EMS system has the role of recognizing that an emergency exists, deciding to act, activating the EMS system, and providing first aid care?

   a. Paramedic

   b. Emergency medical technician

   c. Fire fighter

   d. Citizen responder

2. Which person in the EMS system provides the transition between care provided by the citizen responder and that provided by more advanced medical personnel?

   a. EMS dispatcher

   b. First responder

   c. Emergency medical technician

   d. Paramedic

3. The two body systems that work together to provide oxygen for the cells of the body are—

   a. Musculoskeletal and integumentary.

   b. Respiratory and circulatory.

   c. Integumentary and respiratory.

   d. Circulatory and musculoskeletal.

4. Pathogens enter the body through—

   a. Bites by an infected animal or insect.

   b. Inhaling infected droplets in the air.

   c. Direct contact with an infected person's body fluids.

   d. All of the above.

5. Which of these emergency action principles should you implement first at the scene of an emergency?

   a. Do a secondary survey.

   b. Do a primary survey.

   c. Survey the scene.

   d. Call more advanced medical personnel for help.

6. A victim who can answer your question, "Are you O.K.?"—
   a. Is conscious.
   b. Is breathing.
   c. Has a pulse.
   d. All of the above

7. Why should you do a primary survey in every emergency situation?
   a. Because it will protect you from legal liability
   b. Because it identifies conditions that are an immediate threat to life
   c. Because it identifies conditions that could become life-threatening if not cared for
   d. Because it enables you to protect the victim and bystanders from dangers at the scene

8. In what order are the four elements of a primary survey assessed (first to last)?
   a. Consciousness, airway, breathing, circulation
   b. Airway, breathing, circulation, consciousness
   c. Breathing, airway, circulation, consciousness
   d. Circulation, consciousness, airway, breathing

9. In which circumstances should you move a victim before providing care?
   a. There is danger from fire, poisonous fumes, or an unstable structure.
   b. The victim is complaining of pain.
   c. It is impossible to splint fractures or bandage wounds without moving the victim.
   d. The victim is in a position in which more advanced medical personnel will have difficulty giving care.

10. For which of the following individuals should you immediately summon more advanced medical personnel?

    a. A 22-year-old who has had a fever and vomited twice during the night

    b. A 60-year-old experiencing severe knee pain after a morning run

    c. A 40-year-old complaining that he has felt nauseated, sweaty, and short of breath for at least an hour

    d. An 8-year-old who was hit on the leg by a baseball and now has a large bruise

11. Which should you do to keep the airway open when giving rescue breaths if you do not suspect a head injury?

    a. Lift the chin.

    b. Tilt the head back and lift the chin.

    c. Tilt the head back and lift the neck.

    d. Roll the victim onto one side.

12. Which is a sign/symptom of respiratory distress?

    a. Pale or bluish skin

    b. Tingling in the hands

    c. Constriction of the pupils

    d. a and b

13. What are you accomplishing when you provide rescue breathing to a victim?

    a. Artificially circulating oxygenated blood to the body cells

    b. Supplementing the air the victim is already breathing

    c. Supplying the victim with oxygen necessary for survival

    d. All of the above

14. During which step will you determine if a victim requires rescue breathing?

    a. Secondary survey

    b. Survey of the scene

    c. Primary survey

    d. Preparation for transport

15. What must you do to determine if a victim requires rescue breathing?

    a. Check for a pulse in the neck.

    b. Look, listen, and feel for breathing.

    c. Check for bluish or grayish skin color.

    d. Look at the pupils to check for dilation.

16. When you give rescue breaths, how much air should you breathe into the victim?

    a. Enough to make the stomach rise

    b. Enough to make the chest rise

    c. Enough to feel resistance

    d. Enough to fill the victim's cheeks

17. How can you minimize the amount of air forced into a victim's stomach during rescue breathing?

    a. Breathe slowly into the victim when delivering breaths.

    b. Don't pause between breaths unless absolutely necessary.

    c. Press on the victim's stomach while delivering breaths.

    d. Breathe as hard as you can into the victim.

18. When performing rescue breathing, what should you do after giving the first 2 breaths?

    a. Reposition the head.

    b. Check for a pulse.

    c. Check for consciousness.

    d. Repeat the 2 breaths.

19. If your first 2 breaths do not cause the victim's chest to rise, what should you do?

    a. Call for more advanced medical professionals.

    b. Do a finger sweep of the victim's mouth.

    c. Give 2 more breaths with more force.

    d. Retilt the head and try to give breaths again.

20. What should you do for a conscious adult or child who is choking and cannot cough, speak, or breathe?

    a. Give two full breaths.

    b. Do a finger sweep.

    c. Give abdominal thrusts.

    d. Lower the victim to the floor and open the airway.

21. Where should you position your hands when giving abdominal thrusts to a conscious adult or child?

    a. In the middle of the abdomen just above the navel

    b. On the center of the chest

    c. In the middle of the abdomen well below the navel

    d. None of the above

22. After giving abdominal thrusts to an unconscious adult with an obstructed airway, you should—

    a. Give 2 slow breaths and then do a finger sweep.

    b. Check for a pulse, give 2 slow breaths, and then do a finger sweep.

    c. Do a finger sweep and then check for a pulse.

    d. Do a finger sweep and then give 2 slow breaths.

23. What should you do for a conscious infant who is choking and cannot cry, cough, or breathe?

    a. Give 5 back blows and then 5 chest thrusts.

    b. Give abdominal thrusts.

    c. Give back blows until the victim starts to cough or becomes unconscious.

    d. Any of the above is acceptable.

24. How often should you give rescue breaths to an infant or child who is not breathing but does have a pulse?

    a. Once every second

    b. Once every 3 seconds

    c. Once every 5 seconds

    d. Once every 10 seconds

25. Advantages of using breathing devices include—
    a. Reducing the possibility of disease transmission.
    b. Helping to perform rescue breathing.
    c. Reducing the amount of oxygen in a victim's bloodstream.
    d. a and b.

26. When using a resuscitation mask, the best way to maintain an open airway is to—
    a. Tilt the person's head back.
    b. Lift the jaw upward with both hands.
    c. Keep the person's mouth open, using your thumbs.
    d. All of the above

27. How does a bag-valve mask differ from a resuscitation mask?
    a. It does not help prevent disease transmission.
    b. It is usually more effective when used by two rescuers.
    c. It can be used for victims in respiratory arrest.
    d. a and c

28. Criteria for an effective resuscitation mask include—
    a. A one-way exhalation valve.
    b. An inlet for delivery of supplemental oxygen.
    c. Working well in conditions of extreme heat and cold.
    d. All of the above

29. Which is a disadvantage of the bag-valve mask?
    a. It does not form a tight seal on a victim's face.
    b. It takes regular practice to stay proficient.
    c. It is not readily available to all professional rescuers.
    d. b and c

30. Which is the leading cause of death for adults in the United States?
    a. Stroke
    b. Cancer
    c. Cardiovascular disease
    d. Unintentional injuries

31. The most prominent sign/symptom of a heart attack is—
    a. Persistent chest pain.
    b. Difficulty breathing.
    c. Jaw and left arm pain.
    d. Nausea and sweating.

32. Which action is the most important in caring for a victim complaining of shortness of breath and pressure in the chest?
    a. Providing CPR
    b. Calling for more advanced medical personnel immediately
    c. Asking family members about the victim's health
    d. Calling the victim's personal physician

33. In which position should you place a victim who may be experiencing a heart attack?
    a. Lying on the left side
    b. Sitting or semisitting
    c. The most comfortable position for the victim
    d. Lying on the back with legs elevated

34. Which is the primary sign of cardiac arrest?
    a. No breathing
    b. Dilation of the pupils
    c. Absence of blood pressure
    d. Absence of a pulse

35. The purpose of cardiopulmonary resuscitation (CPR) is to—
    a. Restart heartbeat and breathing in a victim of cardiac arrest.
    b. Prevent clinical death from occurring in a victim of cardiac arrest.
    c. Keep the brain supplied with oxygen until the heart can be restarted.
    d. All of the above

36. When two rescuers giving CPR change positions, they—
    a. Do not change sides.
    b. Quickly change sides.
    c. Omit part of a cycle.
    d. a and c.

37. Once you have started CPR, when should you check to determine whether the victim has a pulse?
    a. After the first 2 minutes (8 cycles) and every 2 minutes thereafter
    b. After the first minute (4 cycles) and every few minutes thereafter
    c. After each minute (4 cycles) of continuous CPR
    d. None of the above

38. During two-rescuer CPR, the person giving the breaths should—
    a. Count aloud to keep the person giving the compressions at the proper rate.
    b. Call for a stop in the compressions after every minute to check for a return of pulse.
    c. Periodically check the effectiveness of the compressions by checking the carotid pulse.
    d. All of the above.

39. When two rescuers are available to begin CPR at the same time, the first rescuer should—
    a. Check the victim's breathing while the second rescuer checks the pulse.
    b. Begin rescue breathing and chest compressions while the second rescuer completes a secondary survey.
    c. Check the victim's breathing and pulse while the second rescuer does a head-tilt and chin-lift.
    d. Do a primary survey while the second rescuer locates the correct position for chest compressions.

40. When a second rescuer arrives while CPR is being given, the second rescuer should immediately—
    a. Replace the first rescuer and continue CPR.
    b. Determine whether more advanced medical personnel have been summoned.
    c. Assist the first rescuer by taking over responsibility for ventilations.
    d. Join the CPR effort by taking over compressions at the end of a cycle of compressions and ventilations.

41. One cycle of CPR for an adult includes—
    a. 30 compressions and 5 breaths.
    b. 10 compressions and 2 breaths.
    c. 15 compressions and 2 breaths.
    d. 15 compressions and 5 breaths.

42. One cycle of CPR for an infant or a child includes—
    a. 5 compressions and 1 breath.
    b. 5 compressions and 2 breaths.
    c. 15 compressions and 2 breaths.
    d. 10 compressions and 1 breath.

43. Where should your hands be when compressing an infant's chest during CPR?
    a. One hand on the chin and one hand on the chest
    b. One hand on the forehead and 2 or 3 fingers on the center of the chest
    c. One hand on the forehead and one hand on the chest
    d. One hand on the chin and 2 or 3 fingers on the center of the chest

44. To deliver chest compressions to a child, you would use the—
    a. Heel of one hand.
    b. Pads of two fingers.
    c. Heel of two hands.
    d. Pads of three fingers.

45. What should you do if a victim's breathing and heartbeat return while you are giving CPR?

    a. Have a bystander transport you and the victim to the nearest hospital.

    b. Continue rescue breathing while waiting for advanced medical personnel to arrive.

    c. Keep the airway open and monitor vital signs.

    d. Complete a secondary survey before calling more advanced medical personnel for assistance.

46. Chest compressions for a near-drowning victim—

    a. Should be given while the victim is in the water.

    b. Are not effective unless the victim is on a hard, firm surface.

    c. Should be given along with rescue breathing.

    d. b and c.

47. For a victim of hypothermia, you should—

    a. Remove any wet clothing.

    b. Warm the victim gradually and handle gently.

    c. Check for a pulse for at least as 45 seconds.

    d. All of the above.

48. When transporting a person without a pulse down a stairway—

    a. Give CPR, then move the victim and resume CPR within 30 seconds.

    b. Give rescue breathing at once but no compressions until the victim is off the stairs.

    c. Get the victim off the stairs before giving CPR.

    d. Give CPR on the stairs until more advanced medical help arrives.

49. You are summoned to a scene where a lineman has received a severe electric shock and is still on the pole. Your first action is—

    a. To bring him down from the pole immediately.

    b. To make sure he is not in contact with the power source and it is safe for you to help.

    c. To give him rescue breathing while he is still on the pole.

    d. To check his pulse.

50. When a victim of an automobile accident is still in the car, you remove the victim—

    a. If the victim is conscious.

    b. If you suspect a head or spine injury.

    c. If the victim asks to be moved.

    d. If you must to provide care.

American Red Cross CPR for the Professional Rescuer
Exam B

IMPORTANT: Read all instructions before beginning this exam.

INSTRUCTIONS: Mark all answers in pencil on a separate answer sheet. Do not write on this exam. The questions on this exam are multiple choice. Read each question slowly and carefully. Then choose the **best** answer and fill in that circle on the answer sheet. If you wish to change an answer, erase your first answer completely. Return this exam to your instructor when you are finished.

EXAMPLE

ANSWER SHEET

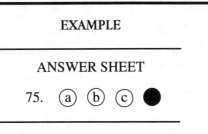

---

75. Why does the American Red Cross teach this course?

    a.   To help people stay calm in emergencies

    b.   To help people make appropriate decisions when they confront an emergency

    c.   To help people in an emergency keep a victim's injuries from getting worse until EMS arrives

    d.   All of the above

---

1. Laws that protect people who willingly give emergency care without accepting anything in return are called—

   a. Citizen Responder laws.

   b. Hold Harmless laws.

   c. Good Samaritan laws.

   d. Medical Immunity laws.

2. Which person in the EMS system has the role of recognizing that an emergency exists, deciding to act, activating the EMS system, and providing first aid care?

   a. Paramedic

   b. Emergency medical technician

   c. Fire fighter

   d. Citizen responder

3. Which body system has the heart, blood, and blood vessels as major components?

   a. Respiratory

   b. Nervous

   c. Circulatory

   d. Integumentary

4. Which body system regulates all body functions?

   a. Respiratory

   b. Circulatory

   c. Integumentary

   d. Nervous

5. How should you determine if a victim is conscious?

   a. Slap the victim's face and ask, "Are you awake?"

   b. Gently tap the victim and ask, "Are you O.K.?"

   c. Pinch the victim's shoulder and ask, "Does this hurt?"

   d. None of the above

6. Before beginning a primary survey, you should first—
   a. Position the victim so that you can open the airway.
   b. Survey the scene.
   c. Check for consciousness.
   d. Call more advanced medical professionals for help.

7. Why should you do a primary survey in every emergency situation?
   a. Because it will protect you from legal liability
   b. Because it identifies conditions that are an immediate threat to life
   c. Because it identifies conditions that could become life-threatening if not cared for
   d. Because it will enable you to protect the victim and bystanders from dangers at the scene

8. In which circumstances should you move a victim before providing care?
   a. There is danger from fire, poisonous fumes, or an unstable structure.
   b. The victim is complaining of pain.
   c. It is impossible to splint fractures or bandage wounds without moving the victim.
   d. The victim is in a position in which more advanced medical personnel will have difficulty giving care.

9. In which order are the four elements of a primary survey assessed (first to last)?
   a. Consciousness, circulation, breathing, airway
   b. Breathing, circulation, airway, consciousness
   c. Consciousness, airway, breathing, circulation
   d. Circulation, airway, breathing, consciousness

10. For which of the following individuals should you immediately summon more advanced medical personnel?
    a. A 22-year-old who has had a fever and vomited twice during the night
    b. A 60-year-old experiencing severe knee pain after a morning run
    c. A 40-year-old complaining that he has felt nauseated, sweaty, and short of breath for at least an hour
    d. An 8-year-old who was hit on the leg by a baseball and now has a large bruise

11. The most common type of breathing emergency is—
    a. Respiratory distress.
    b. Respiratory arrest.
    c. Hyperventilation.
    d. Anaphylactic shock.

12. In which position should you usually place a victim of respiratory distress?
    a. A sitting position
    b. Flat on the back
    c. On one side with head down
    d. Head raised on a pillow

13. Rescue breathing is the proper emergency care for—
    a. Respiratory distress.
    b. Cardiac arrest.
    c. Airway obstruction.
    d. Respiratory arrest.

14. How often should you give rescue breaths to an infant or child who is not breathing but does have a pulse?
    a. Once every 3 seconds
    b. Once every 4 seconds
    c. Once every 6 seconds
    d. Once every 10 seconds

15. When you give rescue breaths, how much air should you breathe into the victim?
    a. Enough to make the stomach rise
    b. Enough to make the chest rise
    c. Enough to feel resistance
    d. Enough to fill the victim's cheeks

16. What should you do for a conscious adult or child who is choking and cannot cough, speak, or breathe?
    a. Give two full breaths.
    b. Do a finger sweep.
    c. Give abdominal thrusts.
    d. Lower the victim to the floor and open the airway.

17. One sign of respiratory distress is—
    a. Pain in the abdomen.
    b. Dilation of the pupils.
    c. Feeling dizzy or lightheaded.
    d. a and b.

18. Which should you do to keep the airway open when giving rescue breaths if you do not suspect a head injury?
    a. Lift the chin.
    b. Tilt the head back and lift the chin.
    c. Tilt the head back and lift the neck.
    d. Roll the victim onto one side.

19. What must you do to determine if a victim requires rescue breathing?
    a. Look, listen, and feel for breathing.
    b. Check for a pulse in the neck.
    c. Check for pale or sweaty skin.
    d. Look at the pupils to check for constriction.

20. If your first 2 breaths do not cause the victim's chest to rise, what should you do?
    a. Call for more advanced medical professionals.
    b. Do a finger sweep of the victim's mouth.
    c. Give 2 more breaths with more force.
    d. Retilt the head and try to give breaths again.

21. After giving abdominal thrusts to an unconscious adult with an obstructed airway, you should—
    a. Begin CPR.
    b. Check for a pulse, give 2 slow breaths, and then do a finger sweep.
    c. Give 2 slow breaths and then do a finger sweep.
    d. Do a finger sweep and then give 2 slow breaths.

22. How can you minimize the amount of air forced into a victim's stomach during rescue breathing?
    a. Breathe slowly into the victim when delivering breaths.
    b. Don't pause between breaths unless absolutely necessary.
    c. Press on the victim's stomach while delivering breaths.
    d. Breathe as hard as you can into the victim.

23. What should you do for a conscious infant who is choking and cannot cry, cough, or breathe?
    a. Give 5 back blows and then 5 chest thrusts.
    b. Give abdominal thrusts.
    c. Give back blows until the victim starts to cough or becomes unconscious.
    d. Any of the above is acceptable.

24. Where should you position your hands when giving abdominal thrusts to a conscious adult or child?
    a. In the middle of the abdomen just above the navel
    b. On the center of the chest
    c. In the middle of the abdomen well below the navel
    d. None of the above

25. Which is a disadvantage of the bag-valve mask?
    a. It does not form a tight seal on a victim's face.
    b. It takes regular practice to stay proficient.
    c. It is not readily available to all professional rescuers.
    d. b and c

26. When using a resuscitation mask, the best way to maintain an open airway is to—
    a. Tilt the person's head back.
    b. Lift the jaw upward with both hands.
    c. Keep the person's mouth open, using your thumbs.
    d. All of the above

27. How does a bag-valve mask differ from a resuscitation mask?
    a. It does not help prevent disease transmission.
    b. It is usually more effective when used by two rescuers.
    c. It can be used for victims in respiratory arrest.
    d. a and c.

28. Criteria for an effective resuscitation mask include—
    a. A one-way exhalation valve.
    b. An inlet for delivery of supplemental oxygen.
    c. Working well in conditions of extreme heat and cold.
    d. All of the above

29. Which of the following is an advantage of using a resuscitation mask to provide artificial ventilation?
    a. It reduces the volume of air needed to expand the victim's lungs.
    b. It prevents airway obstruction from occurring when facial injuries are involved.
    c. It reduces the risk of disease transmission between the rescuer and victim.
    d. All of the above

30. Which is the most common cause of cardiac arrest?
    a. Electrocution
    b. Drowning/suffocation
    c. Cardiovascular disease
    d. Drug overdose/poisoning

31. If CPR is not started, how long after cardiac arrest will the brain begin to die?
    a. Immediately
    b. 2–4 minutes
    c. 4–6 minutes
    d. 8–10 minutes

32. Which of these risk factors for heart disease can be controlled?
    a. High blood pressure
    b. Family history of heart disease
    c. Smoking
    d. a and c

33. One cycle of CPR for an adult includes—
    a. 30 compressions and 5 breaths.
    b. 15 compressions and 2 breaths.
    c. 10 compressions and 2 breaths.
    d. 5 compressions and 1 breath.

34. During two-rescuer CPR, the person giving the breaths should—
    a. Count aloud to keep the person giving the compressions at the proper rate.
    b. Call for a stop in the compressions after every minute to check for a return of pulse.
    c. Periodically check the effectiveness of the compressions by checking the carotid pulse.
    d. All of the above.

35. Where should your hands be when compressing an infant's chest during CPR?
    a. One hand on the chin and one hand on the chest
    b. One hand on the forehead and 2 or 3 fingers on the center of the chest
    c. One hand on the forehead and one hand on the chest
    d. One hand on the chin and 2 or 3 fingers on the center of the chest

36. One cycle of CPR for an infant or a child includes—
    a. 5 compressions and 1 breath.
    b. 5 compressions and 2 breaths.
    c. 15 compressions and 1 breath.
    d. 15 compressions and 2 breaths.

37. When two rescuers giving CPR change positions, they—
    a. Do not change sides.
    b. Quickly change sides.
    c. Omit part of a cycle.
    d. a and c.

38. When two rescuers are available to begin CPR at the same time, the first rescuer should—
    a. Check the victim's breathing while the second rescuer checks the pulse.
    b. Begin rescue breathing and chest compressions while the second rescuer completes a secondary survey.
    c. Check the victim's breathing and pulse while the second rescuer does the head-tilt and chin-lift.
    d. Do a primary survey while the second rescuer locates the correct position for chest compressions.

39. Which is the primary sign of cardiac arrest?
    a. No breathing
    b. Absence of a pulse
    c. Skin which is pale or bluish in color
    d. Absence of blood pressure

40. Once you have started CPR, when should you check to determine whether the victim has a pulse?

    a. After the first 2 minutes (8 cycles) and every 2 minutes thereafter

    b. After the first minute (4 cycles) and every few minutes thereafter

    c. After each minute (4 cycles) of continuous CPR

    d. None of the above

41. The purpose of cardiopulmonary resuscitation (CPR) is to—

    a. Restart heartbeat and breathing in a victim of cardiac arrest.

    b. Prevent clinical death from occurring in a victim of cardiac arrest.

    c. Keep the brain supplied with oxygen until the heart can be restarted.

    d. All of the above.

42. Which is the leading cause of death for adults in the United States?

    a. Unintentional injuries

    b. Cardiovascular disease

    c. Pneumonia

    d. Cancer

43. When a second rescuer arrives while CPR is being given, the second rescuer should immediately—

    a. Do a primary survey.

    b. Replace the first rescuer and continue CPR.

    c. Join the CPR effort by taking over compressions at the end of a cycle of compressions and ventilations.

    d. Determine whether advanced medical personnel have been summoned.

44. The most prominent sign/symptom of a heart attack is—

    a. A pulse which is faster or slower than normal.

    b. Persistent chest pain.

    c. Difficulty breathing.

    d. Nausea and sweating.

45. Which action is the most important in caring for a victim complaining of shortness of breath and pressure in the chest?
    a. Providing CPR
    b. Having the victim lie down while you check her breathing and pulse
    c. Calling for more advanced medical personnel immediately
    d. Calling the victim's personal physician

46. When a victim of an automobile accident is still in the car, you remove the victim—
    a. If the victim is conscious.
    b. If you must to provide care.
    c. If the victim asks to be moved.
    d. If you suspect a head or spine injury.

47. You are summoned to a scene where a lineman has received a severe electric shock and is still on the pole. Your first action is—
    a. To bring him down from the pole immediately.
    b. To give him rescue breathing while he is still on the pole.
    c. To check his pulse.
    d. To make sure he is not in contact with the power source and it is safe for you to help.

48. When transporting a person without a pulse down a stairway—
    a. Give CPR, then move the victim and resume CPR within 30 seconds.
    b. Give rescue breathing at once but no compressions until the victim is off the stairs.
    c. Get the victim off the stairs before giving CPR.
    d. Give CPR on the stairs until more advanced medical help arrives.

49. Chest compressions for a near-drowning victim—
    a. Are not effective unless the victim is on a hard, firm surface.
    b. Should be given while the victim is in the water.
    c. Should be given along with rescue breathing.
    d. a and c.

50. For a victim of hypothermia, you should—
    a. Remove any wet clothing.
    b. Warm the victim gradually and handle gently.
    c. Check for a pulse for as long as 45 seconds.
    d. All of the above.

Answer Sheet: CPR for the Professional Rescuer

Name _____ Date _____ Exam _____

1. (a) (b) (c) (d)   26. (a) (b) (c) (d)
2. (a) (b) (c) (d)   27. (a) (b) (c) (d)
3. (a) (b) (c) (d)   28. (a) (b) (c) (d)
4. (a) (b) (c) (d)   29. (a) (b) (c) (d)
5. (a) (b) (c) (d)   30. (a) (b) (c) (d)
6. (a) (b) (c) (d)   31. (a) (b) (c) (d)
7. (a) (b) (c) (d)   32. (a) (b) (c) (d)
8. (a) (b) (c) (d)   33. (a) (b) (c) (d)
9. (a) (b) (c) (d)   34. (a) (b) (c) (d)
10. (a) (b) (c) (d)   35. (a) (b) (c) (d)
11. (a) (b) (c) (d)   36. (a) (b) (c) (d)
12. (a) (b) (c) (d)   37. (a) (b) (c) (d)
13. (a) (b) (c) (d)   38. (a) (b) (c) (d)
14. (a) (b) (c) (d)   39. (a) (b) (c) (d)
15. (a) (b) (c) (d)   40. (a) (b) (c) (d)
16. (a) (b) (c) (d)   41. (a) (b) (c) (d)
17. (a) (b) (c) (d)   42. (a) (b) (c) (d)
18. (a) (b) (c) (d)   43. (a) (b) (c) (d)
19. (a) (b) (c) (d)   44. (a) (b) (c) (d)
20. (a) (b) (c) (d)   45. (a) (b) (c) (d)
21. (a) (b) (c) (d)   46. (a) (b) (c) (d)
22. (a) (b) (c) (d)   47. (a) (b) (c) (d)
23. (a) (b) (c) (d)   48. (a) (b) (c) (d)
24. (a) (b) (c) (d)   49. (a) (b) (c) (d)
25. (a) (b) (c) (d)   50. (a) (b) (c) (d)

Appendix C

Course Evaluation Form

Date of Course _____ Instructor _____

Location _____

We would like to know what you thought about this American Red Cross CPR for the Professional Rescuer program. You can help maintain the quality of instruction by answering these questions.

Tell us what you thought of the course. (Check your choice.)

	Strongly Agree	Agree	Not Sure	Dis-agree	Strongly Disagree
1. The manual was easy to read.	❑	❑	❑	❑	❑
2. The skill sheets helped me understand the correct steps to take in an emergency.	❑	❑	❑	❑	❑
3. The videos helped me understand how I could use my skills in certain emergencies.	❑	❑	❑	❑	❑
4. The demonstrations in the videos were clear and helpful.	❑	❑	❑	❑	❑
5. I have confidence that I can do these skills correctly.	❑	❑	❑	❑	❑
6. The instructor was well prepared.	❑	❑	❑	❑	❑
7. The instructor gave clear instructions on what to do next.	❑	❑	❑	❑	❑
8. The instructor answered questions clearly.	❑	❑	❑	❑	❑
9. The instructor helped me during the practice sessions.	❑	❑	❑	❑	❑
10. I would recommend this course to a friend.	❑	❑	❑	❑	❑
11. I know when to use the skills I learned in this course.	❑	❑	❑	❑	❑
12. I had to work hard to pass this course.	❑	❑	❑	❑	❑

	Yes	No
13. Was all the equipment in good order?	❐	❐
14. Was the classroom clean and comfortable?	❐	❐
15. Was the facility well suited to skill practice?	❐	❐
16. Did you have enough time to take the written test?	❐	❐
17. Did you have enough time to practice?	❐	❐
18. Did you take this course to fulfill an academic requirement?	❐	❐
19. Did you take this course to fulfill a job requirement?	❐	❐
20. Did you learn what you wanted to learn?	❐	❐

21. Are you:

❐ Under 25 years of age?   ❐ Between 26–55?   ❐ Between 56–75?   ❐ Over 75?

22. Please check the highest level of education you have completed.

❐ Less than high school   ❐ High school   ❐ Some college   ❐ Graduate school

23. How did you hear about this course?

❐ College catalog   ❐ Newspaper   ❐ Television   ❐ Radio
❐ Friend or relative   ❐ Employer   ❐ Pamphlet or poster
❐ Other (please specify)

_____

24. Are you: ❐ Male   ❐ Female

25. Do you have any other comments about this course or your instructor that you would like to share with us?

_____

_____

_____

_____

Thank you for answering these questions. We hope you enjoyed the course.

American Red Cross
CPR for the Professional Rescuer
Instructor Evaluation

To continue to improve this CPR for the Professional Rescuer program, the American Red Cross needs your help. This appendix contains two instructor evaluation forms. Please complete an evaluation form the **FIRST** time you teach the course (photocopy additional copies as needed). Detach and return the completed evaluation (either as a self-fold-and-seal mailer, or by placing a copy in an envelope) to—

American Red Cross
National Headquarters
Health and Safety Course Evaluations
431 18th St., N.W.
Washington, DC 20006–5310

We also invite you to share any observations that you may have about the course at any future time by completing the second evaluation form or by writing to the above address.

American Red Cross CPR for the Professional Rescuer
Instructor Evaluation

Course/Program Information

1. Course completion date ___ / ___ / ___

2. I taught a:
   - ❑ Full length course
   - ❑ Review course
   - ❑ Challenge

3. The total time to complete was:
   - ❑ More than recommended
   - ❑ Same as recommended
   - ❑ Less than recommended

4. Number of participants:
   - In the course _____   Audited _____
   - Passed _____   Failed _____

5. Total number of sessions:
   - ❑ 1   ❑ 3
   - ❑ 2   ❑ 4   ❑ more than 4

6. What was the setting?
   - ❑ Work site
   - ❑ School
   - ❑ Red Cross unit building
   - ❑ Other _____

Instructor Information

7. I have been teaching Health and Safety programs for:
   - ❑ Less than 1 year
   - ❑ 1 to 5 years
   - ❑ 6 to 10 years
   - ❑ 11 to 15 years
   - ❑ More than 15 years

8. I have taught this particular course/program:
   - ❑ Once   ❑ 3 times
   - ❑ Twice   ❑ 4 times   ❑ more than 4 times

9. I taught as a:
   - ❑ Volunteer
   - ❑ Red Cross paid instructor
   - ❑ Instructor paid by a third party

10. On the average, I teach the following number of Red Cross courses each year:
    - ❑ 1   ❑ 6 to 10
    - ❑ 2 to 5   ❑ Over 10

Instructor Manual Information

11. The skill sessions were easy to manage.
    - ❑ Yes   ❑ No

12. The administration information is informative and useful.
    - ❑ Yes   ❑ No

13. The Teaching Tools section provided sufficient information to conduct the course.
    - ❑ Yes   ❑ No

The following information is requested from instructors. This information will help us to learn more about those who teach Red Cross Health and Safety courses/programs. The information will also help us measure our success as we work toward cultural diversity.

14. I am:
    - ❑ Male
    - ❑ Female

15. I am:
    - ❑ White
    - ❑ Black
    - ❑ Hispanic
    - ❑ American Indian/Alaskan Native
    - ❑ Asian/Pacific Islander

16. I am:
    - ❑ Under 25 years of age
    - ❑ 26 to 50 years of age
    - ❑ 51 to 75 years of age

17. I have the following level of education:
    - ❑ Did not complete high school
    - ❑ High school graduate
    - ❑ 2-year college graduate
    - ❑ 4-year college graduate
    - ❑ Post graduate

18. My zip code is _____

over

Optional: If one is developed, would you like to receive a national newsletter for instructors? If so please complete the following information.

Name _____

Your mailing address _____   City _____   State ____   Zip + 4 ____

Red Cross unit name _____
                    (if applicable)

❏ I have submitted my address for the newsletter before.
❏ I have moved; this is a new address.

—Fold here first—

—Tape closed here after second fold—

Information From Participants

Please obtain the following information from the course evaluations that have been completed by participants in your course.

	Strongly Agree	Agree	Not Sure	Disagree	Strongly Disagree
19. The manual was easy to read.	❏	❏	❏	❏	❏
20. The Skills Sheets helped me to understand the correct steps to take.	❏	❏	❏	❏	❏
21. The videos helped me to understand how I could use my skills.	❏	❏	❏	❏	❏
22. The demonstrations on the video were clear and helpful.	❏	❏	❏	❏	❏

Thank you for taking the time to answer these questions. If you have any additional comments about the course, please include them on a separate sheet and include it with this evaluation.

CPWPA/HA
03/93

—Fold here second—

Stamp

American Red Cross CPR for the Professional Rescuer
Instructor Evaluation

Course/Program Information

1. Course completion date __/__/__

2. I taught a:
   - ☐ Full length course
   - ☐ Review course
   - ☐ Challenge

3. The total time to complete was:
   - ☐ More than recommended
   - ☐ Same as recommended
   - ☐ Less than recommended

4. Number of participants:
   In the course _____ Audited _____
   Passed _____ Failed _____

5. Total number of sessions:
   - ☐ 1
   - ☐ 2
   - ☐ 3
   - ☐ 4
   - ☐ more than 4

6. What was the setting?
   - ☐ Work site
   - ☐ School
   - ☐ Red Cross unit building
   - ☐ Other _____

Instructor Information

7. I have been teaching Health and Safety programs for:
   - ☐ Less than 1 year
   - ☐ 1 to 5 years
   - ☐ 6 to 10 years
   - ☐ 11 to 15 years
   - ☐ More than 15 years

8. I have taught this particular course/program:
   - ☐ Once
   - ☐ 3 times
   - ☐ Twice
   - ☐ 4 times
   - ☐ more than 4 times

9. I taught as a:
   - ☐ Volunteer
   - ☐ Red Cross paid instructor
   - ☐ Instructor paid by a third party

10. On the average, I teach the following number of Red Cross courses each year:
    - ☐ 1
    - ☐ 6 to 10
    - ☐ 2 to 5
    - ☐ Over 10

Instructor Manual Information

11. The skill sessions were easy to manage.
    - ☐ Yes ☐ No

12. The administration information is informative and useful.
    - ☐ Yes ☐ No

13. The Teaching Tools section provided sufficient information to conduct the course.
    - ☐ Yes ☐ No

The following information is requested from instructors. This information will help us to learn more about those who teach Red Cross Health and Safety courses/programs. The information will also help us measure our success as we work toward cultural diversity.

14. I am:
    - ☐ Male
    - ☐ Female

15. I am:
    - ☐ White
    - ☐ Black
    - ☐ Hispanic
    - ☐ American Indian/Alaskan Native
    - ☐ Asian/Pacific Islander

16. I am:
    - ☐ Under 25 years of age
    - ☐ 26 to 50 years of age
    - ☐ 51 to 75 years of age

17. I have the following level of education:
    - ☐ Did not complete high school
    - ☐ High school graduate
    - ☐ 2–year college graduate
    - ☐ 4–year college graduate
    - ☐ Post graduate

18. My zip code is _____

over

Optional: If one is developed, would you like to receive a national newsletter for instructors? If so please complete the following information.

Name _____

_____   _____   _____ _____
Your mailing address   City   State   Zip + 4

Red Cross unit name _____
                      (if applicable)

❏ I have submitted my address for the newsletter before.
❏ I have moved; this is a new address.

—Fold here first—

—Tape closed here after second fold—

Information From Participants

Please obtain the following information from the course evaluations that have been completed by participants in your course.

	Strongly Agree	Agree	Not Sure	Disagree	Strongly Disagree
19. The manual was easy to read.	❏	❏	❏	❏	❏
20. The Skills Sheets helped me to understand the correct steps to take.	❏	❏	❏	❏	❏
21. The videos helped me to understand how I could use my skills.	❏	❏	❏	❏	❏
22. The demonstrations on the video were clear and helpful.	❏	❏	❏	❏	❏

Thank you for taking the time to answer these questions. If you have any additional comments about the course, please include them on a separate sheet and include it with this evaluation.

CPRPR/VM
03/93

—Fold here second—

American Red Cross
National Headquarters
Health and Safety Course Evaluations
431 18th St., N.W.
Washington, DC 20006-5310

Stamp

Checklist of Equipment and Supplies Needed to Teach the American Red Cross CPR for the Professional Rescuer Course

For the Class
◆ Viewing equipment: 1/2" VCR and monitor
◆ Extension cord and grounded plug adaptor, if needed
◆ Video—*American Red Cross CPR for the Professional Rescuer* (Stock No. 252051)
◆ Decontamination supplies: decontaminating solution, gauze pads, soap and water, baby bottle brush, basins or buckets, nonsterile disposable gloves, goggles, and any accessories recommended by the manikin manufacturer
◆ Chalkboard, chalk, and eraser, or
◆ Easel pad and marker pens, plus easel or tape
◆ Manikins of each body type (one for every two or three participants)
◆ A box or envelope in which to collect Participant Course Evaluations
◆ Blankets or mats (one for every two or three participants)
◆ Resuscitation masks (one for every two or three participants)
◆ Bag-valve masks (one for every two or three participants)

For Each Participant
◆ Name tag
◆ Pencil and/or pen
◆ Participant Course Evaluation form (Appendix C)
◆ Written exam(s) and answer sheet (Appendix B)
◆ Copy of alternate exam (Appendix B)
◆ *American Red Cross CPR for the Professional Rescuer* participant manual (Stock No. 652048)

For the Instructor
◆ American Red Cross identification
◆ Name tag
◆ Participant manual
◆ *American Red Cross CPR for the Professional Rescuer Instructor's Manual* (Stock No. 652049)
◆ Watch or clock
◆ Instructor Course Evaluation (Appendix D)
◆ Scoring keys for both written tests
◆ Extra manikin parts (faces, lungs, etc.)
◆ Course Record (Form 6418 and Form 6418A)

The Americans With Disabilities Act—Course Modifications Guide

As of January 26, 1992, the Americans With Disabilities Act bars discrimination against the handicapped in places of public accommodation. Title III of the law bars private entities (schools, banks, restaurants, social service agencies, offices, retail sales establishments, etc.) from discriminating against individuals with disabilities in the provision of their goods and services. Individuals with physical or mental disabilities may not be denied full and equal enjoyment of the goods, services, facilities, advantages, or accommodations offered to the public. A place of public accommodation may not discriminate against its patrons, clients, invitees, or guests on the basis of real or perceived disabilities.

There is every reason to believe that the law will apply to the American Red Cross. Health and Safety services, because of the public course offerings and the availability of certification, could be significantly affected. For this reason, every chapter must examine its ability to provide services to a population with diverse needs. In addition, every Red Cross representative who comes in contact with the public or makes decisions that affect the public should be made aware of the law.

For years, the American Red Cross Health and Safety Operations Unit at national headquarters and local units have dealt with individuals whose needs required special accommodation to meet the specific objectives set forth in our courses. These decisions have been based on a doctrine of fairness to the individual within standards set forth in the courses. The Americans with Disabilities Act will require close examination of course objectives and a good faith effort to accommodate, within reason, all those who seek training.

General Recommendations for Instructors

◆ Allow full access to anyone seeking admission to a course regardless of real or perceived disabilities.
◆ Tell participants in every course to participate within the limits of their ability and learn as much as they can. For some people, certification may not be important. For those individuals, focus on helping them to learn as much as possible.
◆ Certify each participant who can meet course skill and testing objectives.
◆ Use available resources to assist people with special needs.

- Provide for the safety of all participants and for your own personal safety. Do not provide assistance to a participant beyond the extent to which you feel comfortable.
- Check regularly with the chapter in whose jurisdiction you are teaching to keep abreast of changes in resources and policies.

Course Modification

The course modification section of this appendix is designed to provide you with insights into providing training opportunities to a diverse population. The courses you teach could include a mix of people who have special needs and those who do not. These courses have been designed to give you the flexibility to train participants who have a wide range of needs and still maintain course standards.

People With Reading Difficulties

If you believe that a course includes participants who have reading difficulties, you should discuss the problem with those participants individually and privately without attracting the attention of the rest of the class.

Identifying People With Reading Difficulties

Whenever you teach a course, you should be aware of the possibility that one or more participants may have reading difficulties. You must be prepared to detect any such difficulties and provide those participants with every opportunity to succeed. Through observation, you may be able to detect that an individual has reading problems. Suspect poor reading skills when—
- A participant says that he or she—
  - Knows English as a second language.
  - Forgot his or her glasses.
  - Has not done well in educational settings.
  - Does not do well in testing situations.
- A participant—
  - Seems nervous and apprehensive.
  - Does not follow along or flips pages as the instructor reads.

The participant in a CPR for the Professional Rescuer course is not required to read material other than the written exam. This exam may be given orally. The challenge for an instructor is to identify participants with reading problems before administering the written test.

People With Physical Limitations

These individuals include those who are hearing disabled, legally blind, lack full use of limbs, or have any other disability that prevents them from participating in a course unless it is specially modified.

Hearing Impaired

The videos shown in these courses are closed captioned to assist those who are deaf or hard of hearing. However, the ability to communicate directions is necessary for a participant to fully take part in course activities. An interpreter should be used whenever possible.

Legally Blind

The success of a legally blind participant who wishes certification in a typical video-based course is obviously limited. The need to touch rather than see demonstrations requires that the participant be given an opportunity to listen to the video and then feel the skill being performed. The integration of touch demonstrations into a course taught by one instructor, within the time recommendations, may be impossible. If special arrangements to provide additional resources have not been made prior to the beginning of the course, you should offer the participant an opportunity to take part in the course by listening to the video and gaining familiarity with the manikins and other equipment. But additional time and resources will be needed to provide an opportunity for success.

As soon as possible, arrangements should be made with your local Red Cross unit representative to provide additional time for a legally blind participant to develop skills.

Other Physical Limitations

Participants with a wide range of limitations may wish to participate in a course. These individuals should be allowed full access to the course and fully briefed as to the types of specific skills required for certification. They must select their level of participation. You may adapt skills within the limit of the objectives in each course component and the text that appears on the skill sheets. Only assist the participant within your personal comfort range.

Do not compromise your safety or the safety of a participant.

Appendix G
Participant Progress Log

Name of Participant	Positioning a Victim, Primary Survey	Rescue Breathing, Adult, Child	Abdominal Thrusts, Unconscious Adult, Child	Abdominal Thrusts, Conscious Adult, Child	Checking a Child or Infant, Unconscious	Rescue Breathing, Infant	Back Blows and Chest Thrusts, Unconscious Infant	CPR, Adult	CPR, Child	CPR, Infant	Using a Resuscitation Mask	Using a Bag-Valve Mask	Two-Rescuer CPR, Beginning Together	Two-Rescuer CPR, Changing Positions
1.														
2.														
3.														
4.														
5.														
6.														
7.														
8.														
9.														
10.														
11.														
12.														

SKILLS

131

Instructor Self-Assessment and Development

Instructors: Using the assessment categories (A, B, C, and D) described below, rate yourself as well as you can on each of the following instructor skills.

> A — Little or no experience in this
> B — Some experience but uncertain degree of skill
> C — Some skill
> D — Good skill

A	B	C	D	Instruction Skills
				1. Planning and managing physical environment (tables, seating, lighting, audiovisual aids, papers)
				2. Setting and maintaining an effective learning climate
				3. Interpreting, applying, and presenting textbook material
				4. Assigning tasks and giving instructions clearly and concisely
				5. Adjusting to group and individual response, and stimulating participation as needed
				6. Managing time
				7. Being able to interpret and implement a Red Cross course design involving the integration of course content, method, and materials.
				8. Evaluating participants' achievement of the course learning objectives
				9. Summarizing material
				10. Maintaining the kind of class discussion that facilitates learning
				11. Bridging effectively—moving from one topic to another
				12. Wrapping up and being conscious of vantage points in the course; summarizing those points
				13. Being aware of my personal image—attributes that add to or detract from my other instructor skills

For other self-development, prepare a development planning worksheet, to include—

OBJECTIVES	PLAN FOR ACCOMPLISHING	RESOURCES

Guidelines for Conducting the American Red Cross CPR for Professional Rescuers Review Course and Challenge

Review Courses and Challenges

Review courses and challenges are opportunities for people possessing current certificate(s) to update their certificates for the course they wish to review without completing an entire course. To teach any review course or conduct a challenge, the instructor must be currently authorized as an American Red Cross Instructor of the course being updated. The instructor should use the same teaching tools in this manual that he or she would use in teaching the regular course.

A review outline is provided in this appendix. Each participant should have the opportunity to view video segments, practice and perform skills for evaluation, and complete the written examination for the course being reviewed. Because this course depends on the video presentation for instruction, the length of the review is reduced primarily by the shorter skill check time required and deletion of lecture and discussions.

A list of completion requirements for the course challenge is also presented. The list consists of skill segments and written examinations that should be included in the challenge. The challenge is intended as an opportunity for a person to demonstrate skills and be evaluated. Those taking part in the challenge should be tested for their ability to perform the skill with little or no coaching. As an instructor, you should provide the participant with signals of the victim's condition and the participant should provide proper care. The length of the challenge is dependent on the skill level of the participant.

Review Course

To be eligible, the participant must—
◆ Possess a current *American Red Cross CPR for the Professional Rescuer* certificate (Stock No. 653214) or
◆ An equivalent American Heart Association CPR certificate (issued within one year)

CPR for the Professional Rescuer Review Course Outline
Length: Approximately 7 hours

Lecture	Introduction to Course
Video	*The Professional Rescuer*
Video	*Human Body Systems*
Video	*Primary Survey*
Skill	Primary Survey
Video	*Clearing an Obstructed Airway—Adult and Child*
Skill	Airway Obstruction—Unconscious Adult/Child
Skill	Airway Obstruction—Conscious Adult/Child
Video	*Clearing an Obstructed Airway—Infant*
Skill	Airway Obstruction—Unconscious Infant
Video	*Using a Resuscitation Mask*
Skill	Using a Resuscitation Mask
Video	*Using a Bag-Valve Mask*
Skill	Using a Bag-Valve Mask
Video	*Recognizing a Heart Attack*
Video	*Adult CPR*
Skill	Adult CPR
Video	*Child CPR*
Skill	Child CPR
Video	*Infant CPR*
Skill	Infant CPR
Video	*Two-Rescuer CPR*
Skill	Two Rescuers Beginning CPR Together Two Rescuers: Changing Positions
Read/Write	Written Examination

CPR for the Professional Rescuer Challenge

Skill	Primary Survey
Skill	Clearing an Obstructed Airway (adult and child, unconscious and conscious)
Skill	Clearing an Obstructed Airway (unconscious infant)
Skill	Using a Resuscitation Mask
Skill	Using a Bag-Valve Mask
Skill	Adult CPR
Skill	Child CPR
Skill	Infant CPR
Skill	Two-Rescuer CPR (beginning together, changing positions
Read/Write	Written Examination

Administrative Terms and Procedures

The following information has been condensed from the *Health and Safety Manual of Administrative Policy and Procedures (MAPP)* (ARC 3530) and is intended to define some Red Cross terminology and give you some background information in course administration. Contact your local unit for further clarification.

Authorized—To be authorized is to be accepted by a local Red Cross unit to teach a Red Cross course in that unit's jurisdiction. When you become authorized as an instructor a chapter representative will endorse the back of your *Instructor* certificate (F–5736).

Certificate—Formal recognition that an individual has passed a Red Cross course of record.

Certified—Term used to describe the circumstance when a course participant passes a Red Cross course and is issued a completion certificate.

Co-teach—Sharing full responsibility and full participation in course leadership with one or more co-instructors; also known as team teaching.

Course of Record—A course taught, properly reported, and accepted by the Red Cross unit in the jurisdiction the course was conducted.

Course Record (Form 6418)—A form that lists demographic information and the grades of participants and is completed by an instructor and turned in within 10 days after course completion to the Red Cross unit in whose jurisdiction the course was taught. This record is used to document certificate issuance, instructor teaching activity, and service activity for statistical reports. May be used as a legal document.

Course Record Addendum (Form 6418A)—A form that lists demographic information on participants and grades received for a course. Should be used when there are more participants than can be listed on the *Course Record* (Form 6418).

Extended Authorization—Permission granted by a local Red Cross unit to a Red Cross instructor from another jurisdiction to teach within that unit's jurisdiction.

Fail—A course grade signifying that a participant has not passed ALL the required skills and/or written tests and prefers not to be retested or does not pass a retest.

Incomplete—A course grade signifying that a participant is unable to complete the course because of certain circumstances, such as illness or death in the family. An incomplete is given only when arrangements to complete the training have been made.

Instructor—A member of a select group of individuals authorized to serve as agents of the Red Cross by teaching American Red Cross basic courses within a unit's jurisdiction and imparting knowledge and skills consistent with American Red Cross policies, procedures, standards, and guidelines.

Instructor Aide—An individual who successfully completes instructor-aide training to help an instructor with a basic course.

Instructor Agreement (Form 6574)—A form to be signed by Red Cross instructors before being authorized to teach a Red Cross course. It explains the rights and responsibilities of both the instructor and the Red Cross unit of authorization.

Instructor Course—On successful completion of an American Red Cross instructor course, you will receive the original copy of an *Instructor* certificate (Form 5736) signed by your instructor trainer. This copy must be endorsed by the local Red Cross unit before teaching. Endorsement by the local unit authorizes you to teach and issue the appropriate American Red Cross certificates within the jurisdiction of that administrative unit.

Instructor Trainer (IT)—A member of a select group of individuals who exemplify the qualities of the American Red Cross and serve as a role model for instructors and other instructor trainers. Instructor trainers serve as agents of the Red Cross and abide by the standards, policies, and procedures of the organization. These individuals are responsible for training instructor candidates in Red Cross specialty areas.

Pass—A course grade signifying that a participant has successfully completed ALL required skills and written tests according to national standards.

Reauthorization—The act of being authorized again by teaching or co-teaching at least one course of record during your authorization period.

Red Cross Unit—A Red Cross unit is any Red Cross chapter, field service territory, or Service to Armed Forces (SAF) station.

Suspension—The temporary withholding of an instructor's authorization by a local unit while formal steps are undertaken to determine whether to continue or withdraw the instructor's authorization.

Teaching Record Card—A card maintained on instructors/instructor trainers that contains general demographic information, Red Cross teaching history, and current authorizations. May be maintained manually or in a computer and is used to determine reauthorizations, awards, and so on.

Transfer of Authorization—The moving of your authorization from one Red Cross unit to a new Red Cross unit in another jurisdiction. Contact your new Red Cross unit for further information on how the Red Cross can transfer your teaching records to your new location.

Volunteer—An individual who, beyond the confines of paid employment and normal responsibilities, contributes time and service to assist the American Red Cross in the accomplishment of its mission.

Withdrawal of Authorization—The removal of an instructor's authorization to teach within the Red Cross unit's jurisdiction for due cause. Due cause, generally, means that the instructor does not or will not abide by the standards, policies, or procedures of the Red Cross organization and its programs or in some way abuses the position of an authorized Red Cross instructor.

Video Calibration Chart

Because there is no standard "counter" on VCR equipment, and because machines can vary slightly in playing speed, you may find it useful to fill out this chart prior to class. It will allow you to locate specific segments of the video for viewing.

Instructions (prior to class)
1. Use the same VCR you will use during class.
2. Make sure the tape is completely rewound.
3. Set the VCR in the play mode.
4. When the first image appears on the screen, set the VCR counter to zero. (The button to set the counter is often marked "Reset.")
5. Enter the counter number at the start of each segment in the space provided below.

American Red Cross
CPR for the Professional Rescuer Video

Segment 1: *The Professional Rescuer* ...._____

Segment 2: *Human Body Systems* ...._____

Segment 3: *Primary Survey* ...._____

Segment 4: *Rescue Breathing* ...._____

Segment 5: *Clearing an Obstructed Airway, Adult and Child* ...._____

Segment 6: *Clearing an Obstructed Airway, Infant* ...._____

Segment 7: *Using a Resuscitation Mask* ...._____

Segment 8: *Using a Bag-Valve Mask* ...._____

Segment 9: *Recognizing a Heart Attack* ...._____

Segment 10: *Adult CPR* ...._____

Segment 11: *Child CPR* ...._____

Segment 12: *Infant CPR* ...._____

Segment 13: *Two-Rescuer CPR* ...._____

Index

Notes

Notes

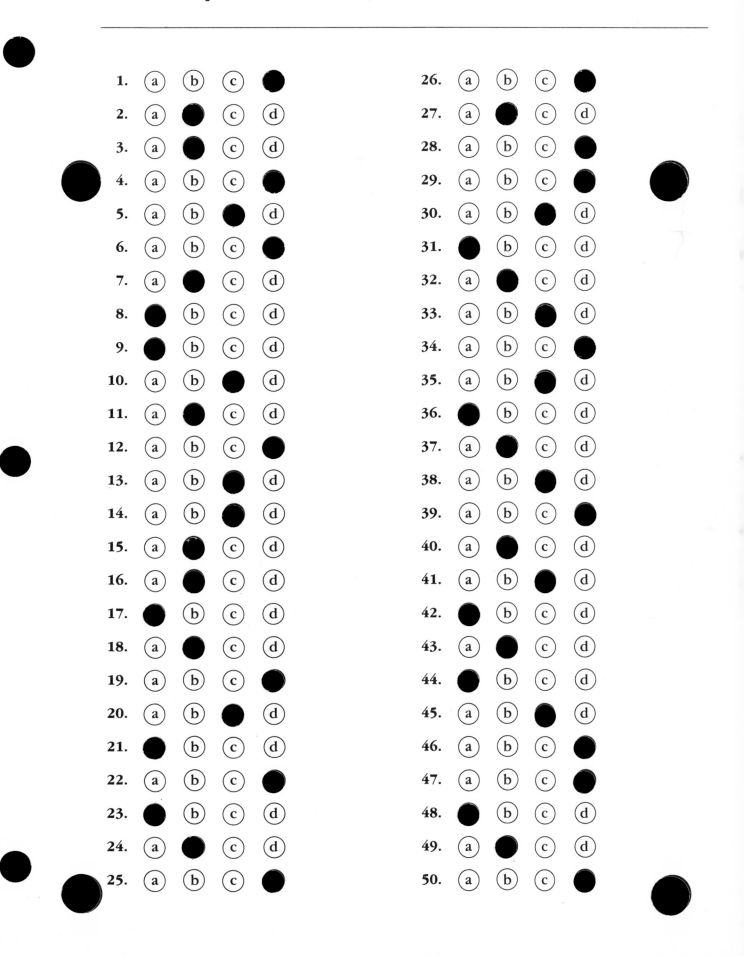

1. (a) (b) (c) ●
2. (a) ● (c) (d)
3. (a) ● (c) (d)
4. (a) (b) (c) ●
5. (a) (b) ● (d)
6. (a) (b) (c) ●
7. (a) ● (c) (d)
8. ● (b) (c) (d)
9. ● (b) (c) (d)
10. (a) (b) ● (d)
11. (a) ● (c) (d)
12. (a) (b) (c) ●
13. (a) (b) ● (d)
14. (a) (b) ● (d)
15. (a) ● (c) (d)
16. (a) ● (c) (d)
17. ● (b) (c) (d)
18. (a) ● (c) (d)
19. (a) (b) (c) ●
20. (a) (b) ● (d)
21. ● (b) (c) (d)
22. (a) (b) (c) ●
23. ● (b) (c) (d)
24. (a) ● (c) (d)
25. (a) (b) (c) ●

26. (a) (b) (c) ●
27. (a) ● (c) (d)
28. (a) (b) (c) ●
29. (a) (b) (c) ●
30. (a) (b) ● (d)
31. ● (b) (c) (d)
32. (a) ● (c) (d)
33. (a) (b) ● (d)
34. (a) (b) (c) ●
35. (a) (b) ● (d)
36. ● (b) (c) (d)
37. (a) ● (c) (d)
38. (a) (b) ● (d)
39. (a) (b) (c) ●
40. (a) ● (c) (d)
41. (a) (b) ● (d)
42. ● (b) (c) (d)
43. (a) ● (c) (d)
44. ● (b) (c) (d)
45. (a) (b) ● (d)
46. (a) (b) (c) ●
47. (a) (b) (c) ●
48. ● (b) (c) (d)
49. (a) ● (c) (d)
50. (a) (b) (c) ●

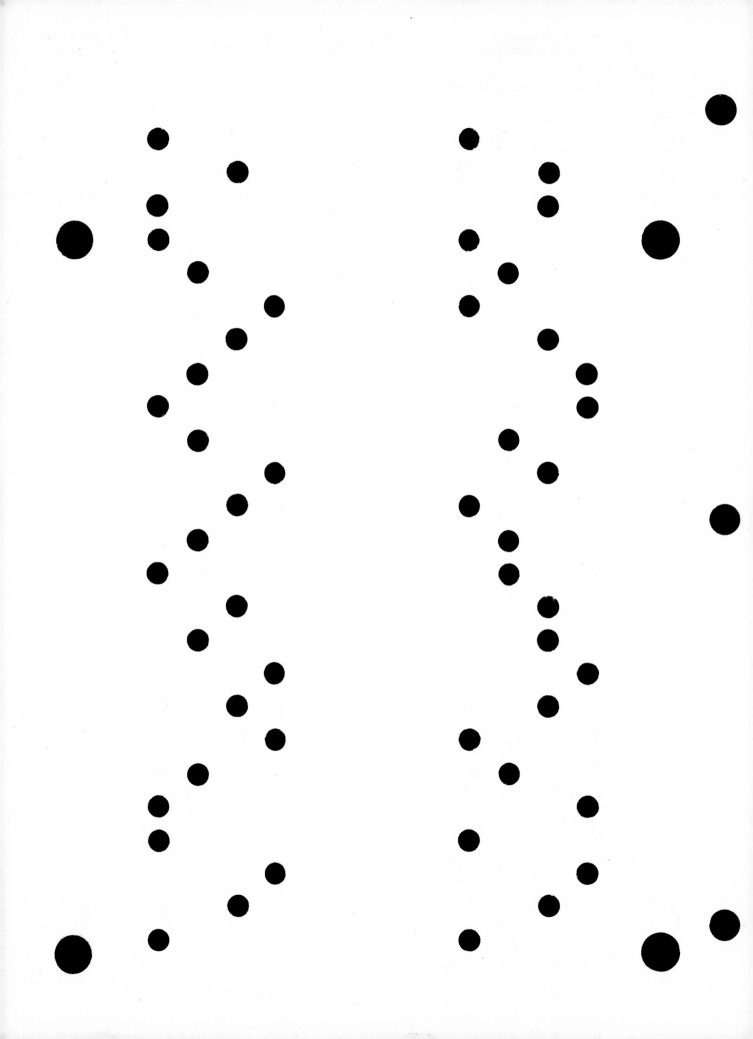